the

Wedding Ceremony

planner

the

Wedding Ceremony

planner

the essential guide to the most important part of your wedding day

Reverend Judith Johnson, PhD

SOURCEBOOKS CASABLANCA™
AN IMPRINT OF SOURCEBOOKS, INC.®
NAPERVILLE, ILLINOIS

Copyright © 2005 by Reverend Judith Johnson, PhD
Cover and internal design © 2005 by Sourcebooks, Inc.
Cover photo © Stockbyte Photography/Veer
Internal photo © Stockbyte Photography/Veer
Sourcebooks and the colophon are registered trademarks of Sourcebooks, Inc.

This publication is designed to provide accurate and authoritative information in regard to the subject matter covered. It is sold with the understanding that the publisher is not engaged in rendering legal, accounting, or other professional service. If legal advice or other expert assistance is required, the services of a competent professional person should be sought.—*From a Declaration of Principles Jointly Adopted by a Committee of the American Bar Association and a Committee of Publishers and Associations*

All brand names and product names used in this book are trademarks, registered trademarks, or trade names of their respective holders. Sourcebooks, Inc., is not associated with any product or vendor in this book.

Published by Sourcebooks Casablanca, an imprint of Sourcebooks, Inc.
P.O. Box 4410, Naperville, Illinois 60567-4410
(630) 961-3900
Fax: (630) 961-2168
www.sourcebooks.com

Library of Congress Cataloging-in-Publication Data
Johnson, PhD, Reverend Judith
 The wedding ceremony planner : the essential guide to the most important part of your wedding day / Judith Johnson.
    p. cm.
 ISBN 1-4022-0343-8 (alk. paper)
 1. Weddings--Planning. 2. Wedding etiquette. I. Title.

HQ745.J64 2005
203'.85--dc22

                                        2004029623

                    Printed and bound in Canada
                    TR 10 9 8 7

To John-Roger and my mother, Grace Mundy,
for teaching me how to love without conditions.

Contents

Part One
Your Wedding Ceremony:
The People, The Place, and Special Considerations

Part Two
Designing Your Ceremony

Part Three
Putting It All Together

Acknowledgments

I am deeply grateful to all the couples who have given me the privilege of officiating at their wedding ceremonies. My special thanks to those of you who so generously granted permission to include your vows and other passages written from your hearts for your ceremonies.

As a first-time author, my journey to publication has been a blessing and an education in itself. Like lining up the tumblers of a combination lock, it has been a process of finding the open doors to bring this book to publication. My thanks to Judy O'Neill for dragging me off to yoga class where I met the lovely Clare Brandt, whose gracious husband Carl, partner in Brandt & Hochman Literary Agents, Inc., directed my manuscript to his associate Marianne Merola, who has become my dream-come-true agent. I am eternally grateful to her for her patience, integrity, and care in placing and shepherding this project. More thanks go to Judy O'Neill for her uncompromising and meticulous care in copy-editing and marketing this book. My deep gratitude as well to Deb Werksman, my wonderful editor, for choosing this project and for not making huge changes to the manuscript. I am also delighted to have this book published by Sourcebooks, a publishing house with a wonderful team that takes such great care in marketing their titles. A very special thanks to Heide Banks for her generosity and support.

And finally, my deep gratitude to my mother, Grace Mundy, and my brother, Bob Johnson, for believing in me and nourishing me with their unwavering love, support, and enthusiasm. After all is said and done, this kind of personal accomplishment would be rather hollow without a cheering section.

Preface

After years of officiating at wedding ceremonies of all kinds, it occurred to me that my experience could be helpful both to couples who are setting out to design their own ceremonies and to clergy who are increasingly called on to perform wedding ceremonies that are customized to the beliefs, values, and circumstances of the couple. There are few hard and fast rules here. When a ceremony is not prescribed by a specific religious tradition, it falls under the laws of the state in which it is performed. As long as the ceremony fulfills those requirements, the couple is free to create as simple or as grand an event as they choose. In a well-designed wedding ritual, there is a certain flow and gathering of focus that crescendos with the exchange of vows, rings, and the pronouncement. As a result, the sequencing of the various ceremonial elements is an essential part of the design.

Over the years, I have collected numerous ceremonial elements that couples wanted to incorporate in their weddings—and have written many myself. As time passed, some couples changed the original writings to suit their own tastes, and it became difficult to track the origins of many passages. I have done my best to do so and I offer these works—original and composite—so that future Brides and Grooms may make them their own.

the
Wedding Ceremony
planner

Part One

Your Wedding Ceremony:
The People, The Place,
and Special Considerations

Setting the Tone for Your Wedding

WHAT IS A SPIRITUAL WEDDING?

When couples come to me to be married, they often describe themselves as spiritual, but not religious. They may indicate that they do not attend religious services of any kind, but consider themselves good, moral people. Most profess a belief in God, though many seek to articulate an image or concept of God that does not match the anthropomorphic God of the Judeo-Christian tradition.

While many struggle to put into words what they mean by "God" or "spiritual," most people agree that there is more to life than meets the eye—that there is a dimension to our being far more essential than our personalities, egos, likes, and dislikes. Some of us call this dimension soul, spirit, or a spark of the divine in us. Others speak simply of something greater than ourselves—something that unites us all. Some think it is love. Whether theistic or atheistic, most of us sense that there is something profound about life. In Twelve-Step Programs, people refer to their higher power, Buddhists seek Buddha Consciousness, and the Taoists speak of the rhythms and flow of life from which they draw strength and wisdom. In many indigenous cultures, this sense of a spiritual dimension of life is often perceived through nature.

When two people who deeply love each other decide to marry, they reach into this essence of their beings in order to create and nurture something greater—their union. In Christianity, Jesus states that he is present when two or more are gathered in his name. This higher union of two beings into one is a universal spiritual concept. The blending together of two people is the mystery of the spiritual union in marriage. At the same time, the two people do not dissolve into one, leaving their separate identities behind. Rather, by giving and receiving their love as they move through their moments, days, months, and years together, they learn to honor and respect their differences, to share their joys, and to love each other through it all with dignity, humor, and compassion.

The spiritual wedding is a sacred ritual where a couple enters into a commitment to take this life-journey of loving, caring, and sharing with each other. Before families and friends, they vow to be by each other's side, no matter what life brings their way. Like an intricate dance, the spiritual union requires that the marriage partners adapt to and maintain balance with each other physically, mentally, emotionally, and spiritually. By being linked together, their lives become a duet where each partner shares responsibility for the quality of the dance they create.

When a couple chooses to be married outside the doctrinal definitions of a particular religion or spiritual path, they have the opportunity to put their signature on the wedding ceremony so that it reflects their individual and combined beliefs and values. Every word, every gesture, can be imbued with a deep significance for the couple. Some embrace this event as an opportunity to build their marriage foundation through public proclamation of their love and intentions as marriage partners. Others have a more lighthearted approach and simply want a heartfelt but nondogmatic ceremony. In either case, it is a wonderful opportunity for self-expression and a declaration of the power of love in their lives.

A good place to start the process of designing your ceremony is to take time together to explore your individual tastes and desires. How do you imagine your ceremony? It is customary in our society for many Grooms to fall into the pattern of saying, "Whatever the Bride wants is fine with me." However, the wedding is as much his as it is hers, so it is very important to support the Groom in discovering and expressing his own preferences. This fact is particularly important in a ceremony that is custom designed rather than one that falls under the authority of a particular religious tradition. Marriage represents the commitment of two people to each other and to their union; it is important that both individuals are strongly represented in order to make the ritual truly reflective of who they are as individuals and as a couple.

Weddings in our society typically emphasize the visual and material aspects of life. We tend to spend time preparing for the wedding celebration rather than equipping ourselves for being married. Some religious traditions offer premarital training programs. But, for those not affiliated with a particular religious or spiritual tradition, preparation for marriage is a "catch as catch can" sort of thing. Television and magazines try to tell us the top ten secrets of a successful marriage. However, it is within our hearts, souls, minds, and bodies that we must prepare to merge our lives with another person—to be joined together by the ties of love, friendship, caring, sharing, compassion, and forgiveness. Marriage is a deeply intimate and individualized process. When you take the time to symbolically and verbally reflect on the very personal meaning of your union through the process of designing your own wedding ceremony, you give yourselves the opportunity to really clarify and share your deepest feelings, needs, and desires with regard to these aspects of your lives. The very act of creating the ceremony can be a sacred journey of expression and commitment to one another.

Your Dream Wedding

In our youth, most of us dream about the day when we will get married and live happily ever after. Our youthful idealism usually carries over into the planning of the actual day. We want it to be special and perfect in every way. The weather will be perfect, her dress and his tux will be fabulous, the ceremony will be touching, the food will taste delicious, the flowers will look beautiful, everyone will have a wonderful time—and the couple will live happily ever after. Of course, this plan does not account for the fact that we live on planet Earth, where things can and do go wrong. Careful planning and preparation are necessary to bring reality as close to your dreams as possible with a minimum amount of stress.

A spiritual wedding ceremony is at once a timeless and sacred ritual and an intricate theatrical production. In both cases, exquisite attention to detail is the key to creating a seemingly seamless flow of events with just the right mood, tone, sentiment, and continuity. When choosing to create your own wedding ceremony, it is not unusual to be surprised by the complexity of the undertaking for what will likely be a mere fifteen- to thirty-minute event. However, it doesn't have to be overwhelming. If you work efficiently, you can work with grace and ease and not be faced with too many unwanted surprises.

Based on the weddings you have attended in the past, you may have a few ideas of what you want or do not want in your ceremony—maybe a reading or a unity candle—and you may know whether you want to write your own vows or use traditional ones. It is perfectly normal not to know what you want when it comes to designing your own ceremony. With good planning and resources, the creation of your wedding ceremony can be a delightful and fruitful adventure.

The Wedding Ceremony Planner is primarily written for those of you who are getting married without the prescribed ritual of a specific religious tradition and want a meaningful, spiritual, and heartfelt ceremony. This book includes a wealth of sample passages to choose from, which will assist you in the creation of your event—ceremony text and sample ceremonies—as well as anecdotal stories and logistical information. It is intended to be a comprehensive resource for dealing with all the profound and mundane details of planning your ceremony.

Part One focuses on all the logistics and special considerations that need to be taken into account regarding the site, placement and movement of the wedding party, and props, musicians, and guests. It provides guidance on how to choose your Officiant and how to find your wedding ceremony location. It also addresses such practicalities as the special issues that need to be tended to in an outdoor wedding and how to deal with loved ones who are attached to their own ideas and beliefs about what your ceremony should be like. Part One also discusses the wedding program and rehearsal. The text is peppered with anecdotes of the wisdom, humor, and sometimes pathos of actual wedding celebrations. This section is not intended to be a primer on the traditional etiquette of weddings and, in fact, will at times break with those practices.

Part Two is the most interactive, as it treats the design of the ceremony itself, from the seating of the guests through the Recessional and all the words in between. It is designed to assist you step by step in creating a ceremonial text that reflects your individual and shared beliefs and circumstances. It also addresses elements of customizing a ceremony, such as including children from a prior marriage, incorporating rituals from religious and ethnic traditions, or having a small and intimate wedding celebration.

Part Three presents additional tools to help you design your ceremony. First, ten sample ceremonies give you some ideas of how all the elements presented in this book fit together. Some couples enjoy exploring what others have done as a way to gather ideas of what they want for their ceremony. Included at the end of each sample ceremony is a Ceremony Text Worksheet that lists all of the elements from Part Two of the book that were used in that particular ceremony. These samples vary in tone, length, and emphasis, and each one reflects the unique life circumstances, beliefs, and values of the couple getting married.

One of the innovations of this book, also presented in Part Three, is that it provides checklists and worksheets to make sure you address all the necessary details and to help you manage and coordinate your planning activities. Samples of completed checklists and worksheets are found throughout the book as their related topics are discussed, and the corresponding blank copies for your use are located in chapter 8. Don't hesitate to send copies of these planning documents to your team of family, friends, and professionals for coordination, and be sure to have extras handy at your rehearsal.

REMEMBER TO TAKE CHARGE

If you are like most couples facing this joyous undertaking, you may not really know where to start or what questions need to be asked of whom. As a result, you are likely to rely on those who are advising you. The problem with this situation is that each advisor is looking through the eyes of his or her specialty, and unless you have a wonderful Bridal Consultant, no one is looking at the whole picture—the overlay of all the different considerations. This predicament is exacerbated by two facts. First of all, the majority of everyone's attention is usually on the reception rather than the ceremony. Second, there are no hard-and-fast rules about who will handle what aspects of the ceremony. For example, the Location Coordinator, the Officiant, or both might attend and oversee your Rehearsal. If there is a Bridal Consultant, he or she will likely attend as well. But who is in charge? Similarly, the Florist may deliver the flower arrangements but not put them in place. Whose job is that? It is therefore essential for the couple to know what questions need to be asked and what options need to be considered to be sure that all goes well.

If you are having your ceremony at the reception location, remember that the way they usually do things may or may not suit you. So, pay attention to the details, such as whether or not you want alcohol served before the ceremony, how the ceremony site will be set up, and privacy for your ceremony in the event that there are other festivities going on there.

Remember, no matter how many professionals, friends, and family members are there to help, and no matter who you choose to officiate, it is important for you to take charge of planning your ceremony. There is no guarantee that the Officiant, Wedding Consultant, or Location Coordinator are going to handle what you think they should. Be sure to ask every question you can think of and put the details in writing so everyone can be aware of your preferences. Probably the biggest mistake is to assume that something will be handled without first making sure that someone considers it his or her responsibility. The most obvious details can fall through the cracks. This book is designed to draw your attention ahead of time to all the aspects of the ceremony that require your consideration. In this way, during the ceremony itself, you will not be distracted by the details and will be free to focus on what really matters—pledging yourself into the sacred union of marriage.

CHOOSING AN OFFICIANT

Years ago, who would marry a couple was pretty obvious because it was common for the couple to share the same religion. Nowadays, people from all combinations and mixtures of religious and spiritual traditions are uniting in marriage. It is the exception rather than the rule that both the Bride and the Groom are active members of the same religion. Many couples want a wedding ceremony that speaks to their shared values without presenting the beliefs of a particular faith. Some know that they want a heartfelt but not sentimental service. Others want a spiritual rather than a strictly civil ceremony. But many couples are at a loss in figuring out who should officiate their ceremony. For those getting married within a particular religious tradition, the level of personalization of the ceremony varies depending on the rules of that particular religion and denomination as well as the flexibility of the clergyperson performing the ceremony.

In the United States, the church and the state are the two authorities governing the content of a wedding ceremony. When a couple is getting married outside the jurisdiction of any specific church or religious organization, they are free to customize the ceremony to their own liking, providing they comply with the requirements of the state in which they are to be married. Check with the local town hall or town clerk to find out what the specific laws are in the state where you will be married. In New York, for example, there are four primary requirements: the Bride and Groom must be at least eighteen years old or have written parental consent; they must obtain a valid marriage license and have the ceremony within sixty days (but not within the first twenty-four hours) of its issuance; their ceremony must be presided over by a qualified Officiant; and the couple must speak their vows in front of at least one additional witness. The rest is optional from the state's point of view. Legally, the couple can merely stand before the Officiant with a guest and exchange vows, be declared married, and sign a marriage license. Of course, most couples prefer to embellish and dignify the event with a more comprehensive ceremony.

According to the 2005 *Encyclopaedia Britannica,* 83.9 percent of the U.S. population label themselves Christians; about 10 percent non-religious or atheist; 4 percent are Hindus, Buddhists, Sikhs, and

Baha'is; 2.2 percent are Muslim; and 1.9 percent are Jewish. We use these religious labels in different ways. Many people identify themselves as this religion or that based on the religion they were raised in, regardless of whether or not they are still active participants. Others are devout practitioners. The fact that an individual calls himself or herself Catholic, Protestant, Jewish, Buddhist, or atheist does not necessarily mean that he or she finds that religious tradition deeply meaningful. Many individuals have drifted away from the religion of their youth and find that getting married raises serious questions for them about their religious and spiritual beliefs. Some couples get caught up in the preferences of key family members and, in an effort to appease others, lose track of the importance of their own beliefs. Many want their ceremony to be free of religious labels—yet tenderhearted and, in some cases, spiritual.

While couples used to be limited to being married in their faith or by a town clerk or judge in the capacity of a justice of the peace, there are now more options. Some couples find themselves surprised when turned away by a priest, minister, or rabbi for doctrinal reasons or because they are not active members of that particular congregation. It is often a rude awakening for the couple. But if they are determined to be married in a specific faith, they should consider looking around to find a more liberal or accommodating clergy member. Some couples choose to have their ceremony co-officiated by representatives of both of their religious traditions. Another option is to have the ceremony performed by an ecumenical or interfaith minister as a neutral voice with whom they can customize the ceremony to their own beliefs.

In the case of ecumenical or interfaith ministers, it is important to check out the scope of religions embraced by these individuals. Some are interfaith Christian ministers, while others honor all religious and spiritual traditions. Many ecumenical ministers, like myself, perform their ministry outside of the context of a church building and congregation and are therefore a bit harder to locate. The best way to find us is to ask your Bridal Consultant or Location Coordinator for some references. There are also regional websites for wedding services. For example, I am listed under "clergy" at www.hudsonvalleyweddings.com. My church also has a website, www.msia.org/ministers, where you can request that an MSIA minister in your area contact you regarding performing your wedding.

Aside from finding a clergy member who shares and/or honors your particular religious or spiritual beliefs, it is also a good idea to find someone who will do more than just read a script. Ideally, you want to feel comfortable with this individual and have him or her serve as a resource and guide in the development of your ceremony and counsel you as needed with any issues that arise. Take the time to determine what matters to you in terms of who marries you. Don't be shy—whatever questions arise in your mind are significant enough to ask. Most couples, for example, want to have a sense of how flexible and creative the Officiant is in the design of the ceremony and how willing he or she will be to work with them. Ask what process the Officiant usually goes through with couples in planning their weddings, and what role he or she typically takes in terms of the Rehearsal and logistical considerations. You will also want to get a feel for the person to see if he or she is someone with whom you are comfortable. And, of course, you will want to know what it costs to retain these services, including whether the Officiant charges a flat rate or variable fees depending on distance traveled, having a Rehearsal, or other considerations.

A PERSONAL PERSPECTIVE

As an ecumenical minister who honors all religious traditions and each individual's right to find his or her own spiritual truth, I have had the opportunity to work with all kinds of couples and marriage circumstances. I work with each couple to help them express their unique style and blend of beliefs in the creation of a ritual that truly celebrates their union. I believe fervently in this right, primarily because I found my own spiritual truth somewhere other than in the religious tradition of my youth, and I have known and been so deeply saddened by religious prejudice. I was not born ecumenical. Having been raised in a Christian faith continues to influence my spiritual beliefs. However, I have been exposed to and embraced many of the teachings of other traditions, most notably Buddhism, Taoism, and Judaism. In speaking from what I know, the reader might detect an emphasis, but not an exclusionary focus, on Christian traditions for two main reasons. First, I live in a society that is over 80 percent Christian. Second, having been raised Christian, it is viscerally a part of me. You will find, however, that the sentiments of most of the wedding text selections I have chosen to include in this book have a universal tone that speaks to the heart rather than to any particular religious tradition—even though some of them originate from a particular religious teaching. In using the material in this book, feel free to adapt the passages to your own beliefs. For example, if you are an atheist and a passage that you otherwise like uses the term "God," be creative in rewording it so it suits you.

I officiate at many wedding ceremonies that take place outside the context of any specific religion. Typically, the couples who come to me are not struggling with differences in belief nor do they deeply identify with any one religion. They may label themselves as belonging to the religion to which they were born, even if they no longer practice it. Most people describe drifting away or intentionally moving in another direction from the religious tradition of their upbringing. Therefore, they find it inappropriate to be married in a particular religious faith and are looking to find a celebrant who will assist them in creating a spiritual tone for their ceremony without representing any one specific religion. Some want to include ritual components of their past or present religious affiliations, but not to be married "in" any one tradition. In some cases, couples that originally wanted to be married in one or the other of their religions became disillusioned by the restrictions they encountered.

I remember one Bride in her forties who had attended the same small-town church all her life and always dreamed of walking up the church's aisle on her wedding day. Unfortunately, when the day came, her circumstances made that impossible. Instead, we created a beautiful outdoor wedding that took place overlooking a river with a backdrop of mountains and a perfect sky full of puffy clouds—and we included as many of her religious rituals as possible. She loved it, yet eight years later, she is still trying to gain permission to have her marriage blessed by her church. I sometimes share this story with couples facing similar challenges in order to remind them how important it is to fully support themselves in their decisions about how to get married. If your dreams and reality cannot be reconciled, do whatever you can to accept your reality and work with it in a loving way.

The decision of two people to live in a committed relationship is one of the most beautiful things that can happen in life. Since most of the couples I marry are already living together, I find their choice to be united in marriage a sacred and joyous cause for celebration. It is a public declaration of love, hope, devotion and the couple's intention to nurture themselves, each other, the relationship, and any children brought into the family by their union. My heart looks past any differences in race, creed, color, situation, or circumstance and I wildly applaud people for caring so deeply for each other. As you step across this threshold together, may you tenderly love one another and yourselves, and be blessed with a safe and happy marriage journey.

2

Deciding Who the Participants Will Be

Remember that your wedding is a celebration of your love and commitment to each other. Always feel free to personalize your ceremony in ways that are meaningful to you. However, be careful that in expressing your uniqueness, you don't become trite. This is your wedding and you do have the opportunity to have it your way, but be sure to consider what your guests' experience is likely to be as well. It is important to balance the desire to personalize the wedding ceremony with an honoring of the traditions that have endured in this ancient social institution. The ideal ceremony is at once private yet public, unique yet universal.

What to Consider in Designing the Ceremony

First and foremost, remember that this is *your* wedding ceremony. Having it "your way" is a declaration of your autonomy as a couple setting off together on your journey as marriage partners. Many well-intentioned loved ones and professional advisors will have lots of opinions to share with you. Whether or not you are the final authority for your wedding is up to you. Just bear in mind that there is a big difference between diplomatically making concessions and abdicating responsibility because you can't stand up to someone with an opinion that differs from your own. I encourage you to be as true to yourselves as possible, assert your authority, and have fun designing the wedding that is right for you.

Before gathering the elements of the ceremony text, there are several key factors influencing the design of the ceremony, including: the temperaments, circumstances, and religious or spiritual beliefs of the couple; the location of the ceremony; and the size and level of closeness of the wedding party and guest list. Reviewing these before actually designing your ceremony will help you to more clearly identify your needs and desires.

The Couple

While we usually think of a wedding as a first marriage and the Bride and Groom as young, this is often not the case. When it comes to the design of the ceremony, there are frequently children from a previous relationship to take into consideration, along with a wide range of personal styles, preferences, and circumstances.

When I meet a couple to explore what they are looking for in a marriage ceremony, I always ask them if they see their marriage more like a straight line or a triangle. Odd as this question may seem on the surface, it is usually understood quite well metaphorically. In the straight-line image, people see themselves meeting another person and going forward on their life's path side by side. Just as in a three-legged race, they link themselves together so that they learn a new sense of balance and find a compatible rhythm. They learn to coordinate their efforts and cooperate with each other. In the triangle image, they see this same relationship, but with a transcendental, spiritual component. They are joined together by something greater than themselves—some call it God or a higher power. There is an element of the sacred present. By joining together, they lift into something greater than what their lives could be separately. Through their commitment to love and cherish each other, they enter into a kind of ministry to themselves and each other in order to experience God's love through their union. They reach into an inner oneness that transcends their external differences, allowing them to know the presence of God in the ordinariness of their lives. In addition, they accept, honor, and celebrate their dissimilarities as opportunities to expand their horizons and know the oneness of God through many manifestations. While it is tempting to say that the latter is the optimal version of marriage, it is not appropriate for everyone. If God is not part of your worldview, then this type of expression does not belong in your wedding ceremony or marriage.

The best way that I have found to really get to know the temperament of a couple is by exposing them to as many different ceremonial styles and approaches as possible. This exposure enables them to find what is true and comfortable for them. They get a sense that "this is us" or "that isn't us." For example, if the partners are shy, they are less likely to want to write long vows to recite during the ceremony. On the other hand, an earthy, casual, extroverted couple is not likely to want a totally traditional and reserved ceremony. To each his and her own. Most often, the signature of a couple has little to do with their specific religious or spiritual beliefs, and much more to do with personal style and approach to life. I have learned not to pigeonhole couples, but rather to allow them to reveal themselves through this process.

I find it fascinating to talk with couples about their beliefs—especially whether or not they believe in God and how that affects how they live their lives. Many couples, particularly younger ones, have had little cause to discuss their religious or spiritual beliefs with each other at any great length, unless their lives are steeped in a religious tradition or if they have faced a major life trauma. A couple may know that he is Jewish and she is Catholic, and the degree to which they practice, but may not have been given any reason to probe this area of their lives further until planning the wedding ceremony. Even for couples who consider themselves to be spiritual but not necessarily religious, the process of designing their wedding ceremony can bring up some unanticipated issues.

This is an area where it is so important for the couple to remember that it is *their* marriage and beliefs that are being celebrated. Sometimes, family members with strong religious convictions may try to impose their point of view on the couple without regard for the Bride and Groom's own personal beliefs. In an effort to keep the peace, the couple can often get so caught up in appeasing others that they lose sight of their own truth and the joy of celebrating their unique union. There are many creative ways to strike a balance without sacrificing your own truth. For example, in one wedding, the Bride's mother was Jewish and the Groom's mother was born-again Christian, so the mothers did two readings in the ceremony: one from the Old Testament and the other from the New Testament. Everyone was happy.

Sometimes, a family member's religious beliefs prevent them from attending the wedding. I ran into this situation several years ago with a young Bride. She was very close to her grandmother, who wanted her to be married in the religious tradition in which she had been raised. However, the Bride was no longer practicing that faith and wanted a ceremony that reflected her beliefs, as well as those of the Groom. The grandmother persisted and refused to attend the ceremony—not in a manipulative way; she simply could not in good conscience attend. I counseled the Bride, encouraging her to talk with her grandmother. Both really needed to listen to one another—regardless of the outcome—so they would at least understand the passion of each other's convictions. The grandmother came to appreciate that it was not appropriate for the young woman to be married in a religious tradition that was neither hers nor the Groom's and gave her blessing to the union. In turn, the Bride made peace with her grandmother's inability to attend the ceremony and wore one of her grandmother's bracelets as a symbol of her presence.

It is extremely important that you and your partner discuss your respective spiritual and religious beliefs with one another if you haven't already done so. Spirituality is an essential dimension of your being, and whether it is currently relevant to you or not, the topic is likely to become more pertinent if you have children. Obviously, it is easiest when the couple shares a similar set of beliefs and religious or spiritual practices. However, if this is not the case, designing the wedding ceremony can provide a wonderful opportunity to practice honoring and celebrating each other's beliefs. In the extreme, this situation can involve having two separate ceremonies and even two separate guest lists. For example, a couple in which the Groom is Hindu and the Bride Christian might choose to have two celebrations: one in each tradition.

The Guest List

Another major factor affecting the design of the ceremony is the size of the guest list and the nature of the guests' relationships with the Bride and Groom. Ideally, you are inviting people who truly matter to you and who you will be able to count on to help you as a couple, if the need arises. However, guest lists have a way of expanding to include relatives and family friends who may not be particularly close to the couple. In some cases, the guest list is largely composed of friends and business associates of the parents of the Bride and Groom, and is often in excess of 150 people. In this case, a couple might be inclined to create a more traditional and less personalized ceremony. If, however, you are planning a small wedding, you might like to look at the ideas presented in the section "For a Smaller Wedding," beginning on page 217.

The Wedding Party

If you are having a small, intimate wedding, it is a good idea to avoid having a large Wedding Party. Imagine how strange it will look to have fourteen people in the Wedding Party and only thirty guests. While it is sometimes difficult to know who to include and who to exclude from your Wedding Party, it is best to err on the side of smaller rather than larger. The fewer people you have, the more meaningful it is for them to have been chosen. Also, consider your pictures. If there are seven Bridesmaids and seven Groomsmen, your photographs might look crowded.

Traditions

There is a fine line between observing tradition and losing yourself in the process. These days, there are as many ways to design a ceremony as there are couples, so which traditions a couple chooses to observe is up to them. Some are societal, some are familial, and others are associated with one's religion or other reference group. For example, some couples like to carry on a family tradition such as wearing the mother's wedding gown, grandmother's mantilla, father's cuff links, or some other memento of a loved one. It can be quite educational for the couple to ask what rituals and traditions have been carried on in each other's families. Some people like to leave an empty chair, perhaps with a rose on it, to remember a loved one who has passed away or was unable to attend.

Perhaps the most universally observed tradition in our country is for the Bride to wear something old, something new, something borrowed, and something blue. Some couples also observe the exchange of very precious gifts between the Bride and Groom, either privately or during the ceremony. I know one couple whose wedding day was almost ruined by the Groom being oblivious to this tradition, which was dearly cherished by the Bride and her family. The Bride had given extensive consideration to her gift for the Groom and had gone to great lengths and expense to obtain it, only to find out that he had no gift for her. Luckily, the Bride's mother was able to console her and help her to see this as an innocent mistake. And the Groom, realizing how much this meant to the Bride, promised he would find a precious wedding gift for her while on their honeymoon. Couples should take the time to find out what is important to each other about the wedding day. After all, this is a day of often unrealistic expectations of perfection, so the more unpleasant surprises you can avoid, the better.

In their quest to be unique, couples sometimes get enthusiastic about including traditions or rituals that do not relate to their own particular heritages; in some cases, they really do not understand them. For example, a couple might think it would be neat to do hand fasting, where the Officiant wraps a cord or ribbon around their hands to signify their union, without realizing that this is actually a medieval ritual of engagement rather than marriage. Or a couple might think it would be fun to jump over a broom at the end of the ceremony. However, this ritual originated in the context of black slavery in America when slaves were not allowed to be married. Therefore, it could be considered highly insensitive for a white couple to jump the broom in a contemporary wedding.

3

Planning the Ceremony Location

In addition to the couple's personality, the guest list, and the choice of Officiant, the location of the ceremony is one of the key elements that will set the tone for your wedding. There are various factors to consider, particularly in the case of an outdoor wedding. Since indoor weddings are a lot more predictable, some of the material in this chapter will relate exclusively to outdoor ceremonies.

FINDING YOUR WEDDING CEREMONY LOCATION

The location of your wedding ceremony sets the tone and first impression for your wedding day. If you are not sure where you want to have your wedding ceremony, there are three keys to finding the location that is right for you:

- Identify your needs and desires;
- Research possible sites; and
- Agree on terms for use of your chosen site.

If you are having a religious ceremony, the location may be dictated by the laws and traditions of your faith. For example, a Catholic ceremony must take place within the church building. If you are free to choose your location, you may want to have your ceremony at the site of the reception, which will streamline the day's activities—especially for out-of-town guests. The Location

Coordinator will be able to show you what options are available for your ceremony site. Be sure to discuss your needs and desires in detail, as the ceremony setup is usually of secondary importance to the coordinator at the reception facility.

If you are planning an outdoor wedding, either at the reception location or somewhere else, be sure to have a well thought out backup plan in case of inclement weather. This could be either a tent or an indoor space. In either case, you might want to have Ushers with big golf umbrellas ready to help guests to and from the parking area and the site. But beware of being too creative. At one recent wedding, the couple rose to the inconvenience of heavy rain by providing beautiful turquoise and red paper Chinese parasols. Although this was an inspired idea, the colors ran off the umbrellas onto all the guests' fine clothing.

Identifying Your Needs and Desires

In selecting a ceremony site, be sure to consider the following:

1. What is important to you about your ceremony location? Is there some special place that has personal meaning for you? Is cost a key factor? Do you want it to be a romantic setting? Inspirational? Beautiful? Unusual? What kind of tone do you want to set for the day?

2. What can you do to make sure your site is user-friendly? This is more typically an issue in outdoor weddings. Some things to consider include:

   • For guests who are elderly or infirm, a mountaintop or long walk into the woods may be an insurmountable obstacle. If such a site is your dream come true, can you provide these people with transportation? In the case of an indoor setting, be sure it is wheelchair accessible if needed.

- Be sure to provide directions that are visually easy to follow to the parking area and from the parking area to the ceremony site if it is not completely obvious.
- Consider the proximity of the ceremony site to the location of the reception. Do you need to provide transportation to and from the ceremony for any of your guests?
- If it is a terribly hot day, perhaps you would like to provide some cold lemonade or water before the ceremony.
- Configure the ceremony site so that neither you nor your Officiant, Wedding Party, or guests have the sun in your eyes.
- If your site is outdoors and off the beaten path, you might want to provide portable toilet facilities, especially if some guests will have driven a considerable distance and the site is not near public restrooms.

3. How important is privacy to you? If you are holding your ceremony in a public place, consider to what extent you will be able to have any control over external noises and privacy, and whether or not that matters to you.
   - If you are being married at your reception location, will there be adequate space between the ceremony site and the area set for the reception or other activities that will simultaneously be taking place at that location?

4. How can you be sure a location is right for you? When evaluating a specific space, consider such factors as:
   - Seating arrangements for the guests—if outdoors, be sure there is a level area for the placement of chairs.
   - What kind of decorations will you need? How will they be set up, anchored, or attached? Will you need tools? Tables? Rope? Tape?
   - Will there be an attractive backdrop for your pictures?
   - Is the space the right size and shape for your bridal party and the number of guests you will have?

- Will the layout enable you to have an aisle and comfortable seating and entry and exit routes for the guests and bridal party?

Note: What may be acceptable and desirable for the location people may or may not suit your needs, so it is important that you talk through these details with them. For example, one location where I often perform weddings has a lovely outdoor gazebo. Several couples, having not explored in detail how this space would work for them, have been taken by surprise when they have found that it can only comfortably accommodate about fifty guests. Therefore, at larger weddings, additional guests end up being seated behind the Officiant, where it is difficult for them to see and hear, and they end up in pictures of the ceremony.

Researching Possible Sites

To find the perfect setting that fulfills all of your requirements, you might want to consider some of the following venues:

- A picturesque outdoor setting such as on a hilltop, by the ocean or a lake, in the woods, or in the desert.
- The home or property of family or friends.
- An estate or historical site.
- Hotels, conference centers, restaurants, or nightclubs.
- An interfaith church, chapel, or other nondenominational religious location. Note: If you are in love with a particular church or temple building, contact the pastor, rabbi, or cleric to see if they are open to the idea of you holding your ceremony in their building with an interfaith minister officiating.
- Retreat centers.
- Inns or bed & breakfasts.
- Golf courses, country clubs, or private clubs.
- Museums or art galleries.

- Yachts or cruise ships.
- Public or private gardens.
- Municipal or state parks.
- Local farms, orchards, or vineyards.
- Catering halls or banquet facilities.
- Lodges.
- Colleges, sororities, or fraternities.
- Somewhere unusual such as underwater, in a hot air balloon, or on horseback.
- Other public and private spaces for rent.

There are many wonderful resources for finding your wedding ceremony site. Here are some suggestions:
- Contact your local tourism board or Chamber of Commerce. Ask for suggestions and look at their brochures of local places of interest.
- Ask around. Contact Bridal Consultants, Caterers, Florists, and other wedding vendors in the area and ask them to recommend some sites. Some Bridal Consultants are available to simply find you a location and are likely to have access to unique and little-known sites.
- Search the Internet. Look for regional websites that give general information about the area and its resources, as well as sites specific to weddings in your area. Once you have identified any specific locations of interest, see if they have a website that can give you more information. There are also national Web directories for finding wedding locations. Most are very useful for large cities and less so for suburban and rural areas. Examples include:
  www.theknot.com
  www.weddingsitesandservices.com
  www.wedalert.com/locations

www.theweddingspot.com
www.thepwg.com (The Perfect Wedding Guide)
www.topweddingsites.com

Major bridal magazines are another great source for ceremony location ideas, particularly for urban areas, and most have excellent websites as well. Some have regional issues that list local resources, including locations. Some state and regional magazines and newspapers also have wedding supplements and special issues. Among the major bridal magazines are:

> *Bridal Guide*
> *BRIDE'S*
> *The Knot Magazine*
> *Modern Bride*
> *Martha Stewart Weddings*
> *Elegant Bride*
> *Today's Bride Magazine*
> *You and Your Wedding*

Agreeing on Terms for Use of Your Chosen Site

When you find the location you like, these are questions you will want to ask:

- Is the location available for your date and time?
- What time can you gain access to the site for decorating and setting up and when do you have to remove your things?
- If you need a tent, chairs, or other items delivered, how do you make arrangements for that with the location?
- What is the cost of renting or using the site and what is included in that fee? Are there any additional fees?
- Who is your contact person at the location? How, when, and where can they be reached?

OPTIMIZING YOUR CEREMONY'S LOCATION

Once you have decided where you want to have your ceremony, be sure to think through the specifics of the actual site you will be using. Again, the location and the ceremony site will create your guests' first impressions of your wedding celebration.

Balance and Fit

On your wedding day, it is important to strike a balance between the number of guests attending, the size of the Wedding Party, and the placement of the Musicians, flowers, and any other props to be used. This balance can be challenging when setting up an outdoor wedding where the ground is likely to be uneven and gusts of wind can blow things about. After all, you don't want the flower arrangements falling off the tables or the guests sliding off their chairs on a hillside! This can be critically important for indoor weddings as well. One location where I have performed many weddings has a wonderful fireplace as the background for the ceremony. However, if there are more than three attendants on each side of the Officiant, this lovely background also includes the kitchen door on one side, and the Groomsmen curving around the corner on the other side. Be sure to consider the fit and placement of all the elements together. For example, you may not want one large flower arrangement behind the Officiant, as it will be blocked during the ceremony. Consider the combined placement of the flowers, Wedding Party, and any other props that will be there. I performed a ceremony decorated with several floral arrangements, plus four attendants on each side of me, and four more holding the chuppah. The space was too small, which made it not only visually cluttered, but also awkward and clumsy for all involved.

If any members of the Wedding Party have to move from one location to another during the ceremony, be sure to take this into account as you plan your layout. For example, many couples like to have a Candle Ceremony that involves lighting candles that are then set into a candelabra on a table. These kinds of movements should be rehearsed to be sure you can move about gracefully, and so all involved know who goes in what order and where each person will be situated around the table. If there are children involved or if there is a particularly large Wedding Party in a small space, it is especially important to rehearse such maneuvers.

If you have readers, consider whether or not to have a podium, which tends to lend a more formal atmosphere. Another choice is whether to have portable microphones for the readers or no amplification of their voices at all. Listening to the readers during the Rehearsal provides the opportunity to give them feedback if they need to slow down, enunciate, or speak louder. If space allows, the readers can stand off to either side of the couple between the Wedding Party and the guests. To minimize the Bride having to move around, especially if her gown has a train, I prefer to place the readers in front of the Groomsmen. Since many readings are directed from the reader to the couple, the Groom can easily move to stand beside the Bride during the readings, facing the reader. Otherwise, it can seem very awkward if the Bride or Groom have their back to the readers.

Special Considerations for Outdoor Weddings

Perhaps the biggest variable in an outdoor wedding is the weather, as it is not guaranteed to cooperate with your plans. If you have your heart set on being married in a garden, on a mountaintop, or at the beach, you need to make peace with the fact that your ceremony may take place in a tent or indoors. I remember one spring wedding where it was going to rain any minute, yet the Bride wouldn't let go of her desire to get married outdoors. She was all dressed and ready to go, but sobbing over the weather and delaying the ceremony in hopes that the storm would pass us by. Meanwhile, the facility people were standing by, ready to reset the chairs and decorations for an indoor ceremony, and the guests were milling around confused, many of them worrying about getting drenched in a downpour. I tried to console the Bride by sharing the folklore that it is good luck to have rain on your wedding day and assuring her that, in the long run, it really wouldn't matter to her at all. By the time she conceded to Mother Nature, it was pouring and the one hundred fifty chairs not only had to be moved, but wiped off as well. It was a mad scramble to the reception tent, and wet shoes on the bare floor made it a bit treacherous to move about with grace and ease. Always have a Plan B if you choose to get married outdoors. Don't let unrealistic hopes overshadow common sense on your wedding day.

No matter what anyone tells you, don't expect to be able to use the reception space as your backup location for an outdoor ceremony—unless, of course, they show you exactly what they would do to accommodate the ceremony and it meets with your approval. It usually ends up compromising the ceremony. Either your guests will end up sitting around the reception tables with no sense of ceremonial community, or they will be crowded into too small a space and the whole feel of the ritual will be lost. Remember that the people in charge of the reception generally view the ceremony as encroaching on their space if it occurs at their site, and their main goal will be to minimize the disruption the ceremony causes to their table settings and other arrangements. You could suggest, for example, that the reception tables can all be set, but hidden behind a room divider until after the ceremony. Hopefully you won't need it, but having a fully developed and viable Plan B well in place for an outdoor wedding can be a great comfort.

Other important concerns about an outdoor wedding are bugs, heat, humidity, and the sun. Bug spray is not my favorite scent, but I have performed many ceremonies where it was a lifesaver. In its absence, you and your guests may be eaten alive, and it is not uncommon for bugs and bees to get caught in the Bride's veil.

For both the beauty of your photographs and the comfort of all concerned, don't forget to take into consideration where the sun will be at the time of day when your ceremony will take place.

I always remind the Wedding Party in an outdoor wedding not to wear sunglasses or eyeglasses with transitional lenses. Perhaps this reminder insults some people, but I know from my own experience that it can happen by mistake. I learned this lesson when I realized after one sunny outdoor ceremony that I had been wearing transitional lenses. Imagine the pictures of the ceremony with the minister in sunglasses!

Many people have difficulty with heat and humidity and are grateful to find that an outdoor wedding is being held under the shade of a big, old tree. One August, I performed a ceremony in the midday sun, and it was about one hundred degrees and unmercifully humid. The sweat poured off the Groom, Best Man, and me. I marveled at the Bride, who was from Florida. She was radiant and did not have one bead of sweat on her, while my glasses were sliding down my nose! Many younger couples or people from hotter climates don't realize how painful the heat and humidity can be for others who simply wilt under such conditions, particularly older guests.

Easily Accessible and User-Friendly

Remember that the comfort of your guests is important. You might want to forego your dream of a ceremony in a remote location in favor of making it possible for your guests to get there. There is also the consideration of bathroom facilities. While most ceremonies are less than half an hour, your guests may be there for an hour or more from arrival to departure. If you have to resort to port-o-potties, see if you can find some discreet way to place them so guests know where they are but they don't end up in your pictures. One couple got married in their own garden, and their house did not have adequate plumbing to accommodate all the guests. At the entrance to the woods on the edge of their property, they constructed a fake wall to create the illusion of a door and put a "Men's Room" sign on it. This may not fit your taste, but in their case, it was a wonderfully creative solution.

When all of these matters are taken into account, you can relax and enjoy your wedding. But remember, one thing that a wedding always requires is a sense of humor. Things can and do go wrong when you least expect it, so expect the unexpected, and make room for serendipity.

FACTORS TO CONSIDER IN DESIGNING THE CEREMONY SITE

Now that we've introduced the basics, we can go into great detail about how to plan the site where your ceremony will take place. Ceremony site planning is one of the most essential steps in creating a hassle-free ceremony. It gives you the opportunity to think of all the elements of your ceremony together to be sure that it will all work simultaneously. Don't leave this planning to someone else's discretion until you have first given it some thought. Let the experts give you their input, but you decide. Review all the details and options to see what matters to you and what does not. Then, communicate with everyone involved and delegate tasks appropriately.

As you meet with your Florist, Musicians, Officiant, and other professionals, it is important to think about how all these various elements are going to work together. To help you with this, a sample Ceremony Site Layout Worksheet follows; a blank one for your use can be found on page 352.

Ceremony Site Layout Worksheet—Sample

Describe exactly how the ceremony site will be set up, including the location of all flowers, decorations and props, Musicians, Readers, the Officiant, Wedding Party members, chairs, and so on. Describe them all in relationship to each other.

Chairs:

• *There will be fifteen straight rows of chairs on each side of the center aisle facing the window in the Parlor Room.*

• *Each row on each side will have six chairs for a total of 180 chairs.*

• *The first two rows on the left and right will be reserved seats as follows (from left to right):*
Bride's side—left (facing altar)

Row 1:

Row 2:

Groom's side—right (facing altar)

Row 1:

Row 2:

Flowers, Decorations and Props:

• *A floral arch will be placed about fifteen feet in front of the first row, anchored by four stakes.*

• *There will be a table in front of the Bridesmaids with a bouquet of flowers centered at the back and a candelabra centered in front. The center candle will be in the candelabra and the two side candles will be laying on the table in front of the candelabra. A small box of wooden matches will be next to the two candles. There will also be flower petals sprinkled on the table.*

• *A large pedestal floral arrangement will be placed at the outside end of the row of Bridesmaids and another at the end of the Groomsmen.*

Officiant and Wedding Party:

• *The Officiant will stand under the floral arch facing the guests.*

• *Bride and Groom stand facing each other in front of the Officiant. The Bride is on the left (facing the altar) and the Groom is on the right.*

• *Maid of Honor and Best Man stand on the right and left sides of the Officiant respectively, angled toward the couple.*

• *Three Bridesmaids and three Groomsmen stand beside the Maid of Honor and Best Man respectively, all angled toward the couple.*

• *The Flower Girl will stand in front of the first Bridesmaid and the Ring Bearer will stand in front of the first Groomsman.*

Musicians:
- *The piano will be in the front left corner of the room, with space in front of it for the other three Musicians. (The area is equipped with all of the electrical outlets that will be needed.)*

Readers:
- *A podium with a microphone will be located halfway between the Groomsmen and the guests on the right-hand side, angled slightly toward the Bride and Groom.*

Photographer:
- *The Photographer and Officiant have discussed the logistics of the ceremony.*
- *The ceremony will be videotaped from the center aisle behind the guests and the Videographer will move off to the side of the aisle during the Processional and Recessional.*

Other:
- *The Officiant will have a portable microphone.*

With the Ceremony Site Layout Worksheet—Sample as a reference point, consider how you want to customize each of the following features for your wedding ceremony.

The Wedding Party

A good place to start in planning the ceremony site is with the placement of the Officiant and the Wedding Party. While many people are used to ceremonies where the Bride and Groom and Wedding Party have their backs to the guests, others find this awkward. When the Bride and Groom face each other in front of the Officiant with the Wedding Party at the Officiant's side facing the couple and the guests, a more intimate feeling is created. That way the guests can see everyone. One caveat here though is that, with guests seated on the traditional Bride's and Groom's sides, those on the Bride's side will have a front view of the Groom and a back view of the Bride and vice versa. Some couples choose to have the Officiant stand with his or her back to the guests, and the couple facing the guests. But, given the fact that the Officiant is the one who is speaking to both the couple and the guests for the majority of the ceremony, this can be an awkward arrangement as well. So, think through what placement of the Wedding Party is most comfortable and appropriate for you.

Props

With the Wedding Party in place, now lay in the props. Where will the floral arrangements go? Will they be on tables, pedestals, or freestanding? Do they need to be secured against a good gust of wind? Where will the readers stand? Think through all the movements that will take place during the ceremony to consider any props that might be needed. For example, many couples choose to have a Candle Ceremony. If the candelabra is located on a table to the Officiant's right in front of the Bridesmaids, then it will be easier for the Bride's attendants to help her with her flowers and the train on her dress should she need assistance. Consider how you want such a table decorated. Do you want a tablecloth? Flowers? Be sure to have wooden matches or a wand lighter handy for a Candle Ceremony. At a recent wedding, one of my acrylic nails melted when trying to prelight the candles with a small lighter on a windy day. If you will be doing a water or wine ceremony, you will want to provide a table near the Officiant for the water or wine and a glass. It is also a good idea to have a glass of water handy for the Officiant, particularly in hot weather.

If you are going to need sound equipment to amplify the Officiant, couple, Readers, and/or Musicians, be sure to think through how, where, and when that will be handled. Also, be sure all wires are out of the way of the ceremony activities and taped securely to the floor or ground if possible. Similarly, if you are going to have your ceremony videotaped, check out any considerations the Officiant may have regarding videotaping and photography of the ceremony. Then, discuss your plans with the person doing the taping in terms of where you want him or her to stand to get the best view. Ask the Photographer and Officiant to touch base with each other on the wedding day itself. Most photographers are highly experienced at getting great pictures while being unobtrusive. I have met a few, though, over whom I practically had to crawl to move around the ceremony site. On one occasion, the Photographer delayed the ceremony by one hour during a hurricane because he insisted on doing the formal photographs before the ceremony. Not only did this deprive the couple of fulfilling their desire to not see each other before the ceremony, but all the guests were at the bar and no one from the facility was paying attention to the guests who were entering the ceremony room with their drinks in hand.

Finally, don't forget an essential prop—tissues. You never know who might cry, so you might want the Groom and Best Man to have some tissues in their pockets. Bridesmaids can usually hold tissues behind their bouquets.

Chairs

Many people think they can do without chairs to create a more intimate and casual tone for a small wedding. Please do have chairs. Chairs are a godsend to more guests than you would expect, plus they provide order and focus. At one wedding where the couple insisted on having no chairs, a number of guests chose to smoke, drink, and talk under a tree about thirty feet from the ceremony site during the wedding. You may think that your guests would never behave this way, but neither did this couple. You'd be surprised what some people do. With chairs, you can do your best to guide and direct your guests in accordance with your plans and preferences.

You can create greater intimacy by arranging the chairs in curved rows or, for very small ceremonies, in a semicircle. At a larger wedding, slightly curved rows create a warmer feeling and greater focus for guests. If chairs will not be available for all guests, you may want to consider having at least a few rows with an aisle for immediate family and older or infirm guests. Be sure to identify how many seats you need to reserve for family members, readers, and others, and specify where these seats will be placed. Notify those with reserved seats ahead of time exactly where their seats will be, especially if you have divorced parents who will be present with their new partners. If you have young children in your Wedding Party, you might want to have their parents or close relatives seated in the front row so the children can easily go to them if needed. Some couples choose to have the children process and recess, but sit with their parents during the ceremony. Be sure to practice this with the children at the Rehearsal so they know what to expect. And, of course, be sure to discuss your seating plans with the Ushers so they know if you are having a Bride's side and a Groom's side, which seats are reserved, and who is to be seated where.

In planning the number of chairs and rows, take into account the shape of the available space and the ease with which guests will be able to enter and exit their seats. If you have decorative covers on the chairs, for example, you will want to allow more space between rows.

While many couples like to have a designated Bride's and Groom's side for seating the guests, some couples prefer mixed seating, particularly if one side has many more guests than the other. But even with mixed seating, you will probably want to have reserved seating for immediate family in the traditional location of the front rows. If the ceremony is taking place in a church or temple, be sure to discuss with the clergy your preferences regarding the seating of guests and any decorations you have in mind. Be sensitive to their rules and beliefs. For example, some might allow you to put decorations on the end of each pew and others may not.

Music

Music is an essential ingredient in the design of the ceremony. Consider the impact on the tone of the ceremony if you were to have a string quartet, a harpist, trumpets, or bagpipes. Typically, couples choose musical selections for three specific parts of the ceremony: the seating of the guests, the Processional, and the Recessional. During the Processional, you may want two distinct selections—one for the Wedding Party and a second for the Bride.

A ceremony without music tends to have an empty feeling. Music provides a cushiony container within which the ritual occurs. It sets the tone and puts everyone at ease. It also harmonizes everyone together. Having music playing while the guests are being seated creates the mood and gives them a sense of things having already started, rather than waiting for them to begin. Music has a relaxing effect.

Some couples try to save money by using taped music for the ceremony. No matter how wonderful your selections and your sound system are, this almost never works. The one exception I've seen was with a very conservative couple. Unbeknownst to me, the Groom had a passion for James Brown's music. When I pronounced them husband and wife and they kissed, James Brown's "I Feel Good" blared out from the back of the room as the Recessional music while they danced down the aisle together. It was a truly fantastic moment! However, with taped music, often either the person working the equipment misses his or her cue by a split second or the beginning of the tape takes a few moments to get to the music and it feels like an awkward eternity. If you do plan to use taped music, rehearse the exact timing with the person who will be playing it during your ceremony. This way, any mishaps can be worked through at the Rehearsal. If the music is live, it is much easier to adapt the music to the pace of the Processional and Recessional. If at all possible, use live music and save money somewhere else.

If you have friends who are musicians and you want to feature them in the ceremony itself, you may want to consider several factors. Even if the musicians are excellent, the guests often lose their focus during a purely instrumental piece. Also, it can be awkward for the Bride, Groom, and Wedding Party to stand there watching the musicians. Perhaps a better choice would be to have them play during the seating of the guests or be featured during the reception. With a vocalist, it's more comfortable, especially if they love what they are singing and the lyrics tie into the sentiment of the ceremony.

I remember one wedding where the Bride and Groom both came from musical families. The couple's family members escorted the guests to the ceremony site in a kind of whimsical parade and back again at the end of the ceremony to where the receiving line would be. It added a wonderful sense of family, frivolity, and joy to the ceremony.

Some couples wonder if they should have music softly playing in the background during the entire ceremony or during a symbolic ritual such as the Candle Ceremony. This can be distracting and makes it difficult to strike a balance between the ritual, the text, and the music. It ends up feeling like simultaneous, but discreet activities rather than a synergistic whole. My experience shows that music is most effective when used only for the seating of the guests, the Recessional, and the Processional. A single, short vocal piece can be nice as well. However, vocal and instrumental performances can often be more effectively incorporated in the wedding reception.

The following is a partial list of some of the more popular musical selections used for wedding ceremonies:

- Antonio Vivaldi—Largo (*Winter—The Four Seasons*)
- Johann Sebastian Bach—Air on the G String (*Suite in D*)
- Claude Debussy—"Clair de Lune"

- Wolfgang Amadeus Mozart—Romance
  (*Eine kleine Nachtmusik*)
- Antonio Vivaldi—Adagio (*Mandolin Concerto in D*)
- Pietro Mascagni—Intermezzo (*Cavalleria Rusticana*)
- Medley: Jeremiah Clarke—Trumpet Voluntary; Jean-Joseph
  Mouret—Rondeau; George Frideric Handel—
  "La Rejouissance" (*Music for the Royal Fireworks*);
  Handel—"Hornpipe" (*Water Music*)
- Johann Pachelbel—Canon in D
- Richard Wagner—Bridal Chorus (*Lohengrin*)
- Franz Shubert—"Ave Maria"
- Cesar Franck—"Panis Angelicus" (O Lord Most Holy)
- Felix Mendelssohn Bartholdy—Wedding March
  (*A Midsummer's Night Dream*)
- Luigi Boccherini—Menuet
- Christoph Gluck—Melody (*Orfeo*)
- Robert Schumann—"Traumerei"

Special Considerations

Sometimes, enormous diplomacy is necessary to bridge the different worlds that are being united by the union of a man and a woman in marriage. There are times when the couple, in order to claim the space in this world for their union, must willingly go into some dicey territory. It is best for the couple to anticipate and address whatever emotional, dogmatic, or ideological conflicts might arise that could put a damper on their day. There are obvious limits to this, but it is important to at least deal with known issues within families. Conflicts are part of the initiation process of marriage. Consider the couple who avoided telling her conservative parents that the Groom's mother was a lesbian and would attend the wedding with her partner. As it turned out, the Bride's father and Groom's mother and her partner met at the Rehearsal, creating an unnecessarily awkward moment for all of them. So, don't avoid potentially difficult family issues or situations. Instead, be brave and address them head-on.

"HANDLE WITH CARE" RELATIONSHIPS

Remember that, with the exception of the Rehearsal and Rehearsal Dinner that are usually attended by your family and Wedding Party, the ceremony may be the first official gathering of your guests.

As such, there may be some awkward encounters. For example, perhaps the Bride's or Groom's parents are divorced and not on good terms. Be sure to discuss with them ahead of time how you want them to behave when they encounter one another, their seating, and how important it is to you that they do whatever they can to avoid conflict on your day. At one Wedding Rehearsal, the Bride's stepmother felt slighted by where she was assigned to sit at the wedding. She took her revenge by disappearing just before the ceremony. The Bride's father did not want to walk his daughter up the aisle until he knew where his wife was and that she was all right. I had already been given the cue to take my place along with the Groom and Groomsmen. We ended up waiting fifteen minutes while they searched for her. Finally, she emerged from the parking area and sat in the back instead of in her assigned seat in the second row. She had made her point.

If this is a second marriage and there are children from previous marriages involved, it is very important to think through the appropriate way to include them. This is discussed in Part Two beginning on page 61. If in their teens or twenties, children may feel that they have to take sides with one parent or the other, or that the marrying parent is somehow betraying the single parent. Even if the children say they are OK with it, create the opportunity to have discussions that give them the chance to go below the surface of their feelings. Once aired, they can move beyond concerns of loyalty to one parent or the other and take on a larger view of the situation. If a child is uncomfortable participating in your wedding, honor that. They have a right to feel however they do. Be sensitive to their needs but remember that it is your day.

Sometimes, it is appropriate in the ceremony to place as much emphasis on the creation of a new family as on the marriage of the Bride and Groom, which helps children feel included and not just like supplementary baggage. Remember that no matter how well-adjusted your children are, your commitment to a new spouse is usually interpreted as your having less time or attention for them. It also is a tough reminder for many children of the fragility of love, and many fear that you will stop loving them as you did their other parent.

Sometimes, the blending of the couple's parents involves bridging a culturally wide gap. In one wedding, the Bride was Japanese and the Groom was Irish Catholic. Her parents and two uncles flew to the States for the wedding, but none of them spoke English. The Bride's father was elderly and in a wheelchair, so her mother walked her up the aisle. When we were rehearsing the Bride's arrival at the ceremony site, it took about half an hour to negotiate how the Groom should address the mother when coming to meet the Bride. It was deemed inappropriate for him to shake the mother's hand or to hug her as he would do in his own culture. Instead, it was agreed that he would bow at a particular angle to the mother and she to him. It was very touching.

When there are two primary languages spoken among the guests, consider having a translator to echo the Officiant. Translations can be done with both spoken and sign language. In both cases, it can be very moving for all involved. This idea can be used to clarify a portion of the ceremony as well. For example, when incorporating components of a particular religious tradition in the ceremony, it can be very meaningful to have someone steeped in the faith of that tradition to officiate. If the couple speaks a different language than the Officiant, it might be appropriate to have a translator and for the couple to take a few moments to communicate to each other in their native language before the start of the ceremony and after exchanging the Wedding Vows.

Who Does What, When, Where, Why, and How
The good news about designing your own wedding ceremony is that you get to have it your way. The bad news is you have to figure out

what that is and how to make it happen. In a traditional religious ceremony, years of repetition have clarified who will do what, when, where, why, and how. But creating your own ceremony puts you in virgin territory. You may gather ideas from various places, but when you put it all together, it will be unique; roles and transitions will have to be thought through. Keep handy a central list of all your essential contacts for your wedding so you can coordinate between them more easily and share information more efficiently. A sample Wedding Day Information Sheet follows and a blank copy for your use is on page 353.

While it is usually pretty straightforward who is in charge of what for the wedding reception, it is not so easy to determine who handles what aspect of the ceremony itself. Many couples assume the Officiant, Bridal Consultant, or Location Coordinator will know what needs to be done and will take care of it. However, skills, abilities, preferences, and inclinations vary widely as to how individuals perform these roles. And, despite the fact that the entire wedding day is really about the exchange of vows between the couple, most people focus most of their attention on everything but the ceremony itself. Often a Bridal Consultant or Location Coordinator will reassure the couple from the beginning that they don't have to worry about a thing, that everything will be taken care of for them. In some cases, this is delightfully so, but until you are sure that you are in wonderfully competent hands, make no assumptions about who will do what, other than the really obvious things like the Officiant performing the actual ceremony. Think through all the minutia and carefully decide exactly how you want each aspect of your ceremony handled. Then put your plans in writing, delegate, and gracefully let people know what you are counting on them to do.

One good rule of thumb is to be sure that for each thing you choose to do, you ask yourselves: How exactly do we want this done, and by whom? For example, if someone has a baby or young child

Wedding Day Information Sheet—Sample

Ceremony Location: *Mohonk Mountain House - Second Floor Parlor Room*
Rehearsal (Date and Time): *Friday, August 10 at 5 p.m.*
Ceremony (Date and Time): *Saturday, August 11 at 5 p.m.*

Participants/Resources	Name	Phone	Email
Bride	*Barbara Jones*	*123-456-7890*	*abc@def.com*
Groom	*William Johnson*	*123-456-7890*	*abc@def.com*
Officiant	*Rev. Judith Johnson*	*123-456-7890*	*abc@def.com*
Maid of Honor	*Cynthia Schneider*	*123-456-7890*	*abc@def.com*
Best Man	*Jacob Feagan*	*123-456-7890*	*abc@def.com*
Bridal Consultant	*Daphne Burrows*	*123-456-7890*	*abc@def.com*
Location Coordinator	*Stephen Adams*	*123-456-7890*	*abc@def.com*
Caterer	*Feast Inc.*	*123-456-7890*	*abc@def.com*
Florist	*Flower Power*	*123-456-7890*	*abc@def.com*

coming to the ceremony, discuss options with them of what to do if the child starts to cry or becomes a distraction during the ceremony. The child's parents may have different ideas about this than you do. Another example would be using an aisle runner. Who will be in charge of the runner (be sure to have two people) and exactly when do you want them to unroll it? If you are not attentive, it may be rolled out for the entire Wedding Party instead of just for the Bride. Innocent errors can occur because many people do not know the meaning behind the rituals and therefore don't know the significance of their actions.

In most cases, no matter how carefully you have planned the ceremony, there will be unexpected last-minute details that need to be decisively handled. One way or the other, it is important to make sure that someone is given a checklist and the job of checking out the ceremony site a half hour before the ceremony begins to be sure that everything is where it should be. Sometimes it is necessary to move tables, chairs, and floral arrangements that have been improperly placed. Don't be shy about assigning these tasks, and about making your own checklist and giving it to the Coordinator, a member of the Wedding Party, or a family member. Do not assume that anything will be automatically handled. See the Just Before the Ceremony Checklist that follows. A blank one is available for your use on page 354.

Consider the wedding where there were two floral arrangements in tall, top-heavy wicker stands that were to be situated beside the Wedding Party. The Florist had tied them with rope to the tree that would be the ceremony backdrop. The Maid of Honor, father of the Bride, one of the Musicians, and the Location Coordinator all noticed this and puzzled over how to secure them so they would not fall over. They untied them from the tree and, no matter where they placed them, it was clear that they would tip over with the slightest breeze. No one knew what to do and the ceremony was

Just Before the Ceremony Checklist—Sample

List everything that needs a final check to ensure that all goes smoothly.
Indicate who will check which items.

Activity	Person Responsible
1. Does the Groom have the cards with the vows in his pocket?	Bridal Consultant
2. Does the Best Man have the rings?	Bridal Consultant
3. Has the ceremony site layout been checked? (Check all details listed on Your Ceremony Site Layout Worksheet.)	Bridal Consultant and Bride's sister
4. Do the Ushers all know which family members they are escorting, in what sequence, and where to seat them?	Best Man
5. Does the Officiant have the marriage license?	Bridal Consultant
6. Has the Officiant reviewed the ceremony with the Photographer and Musicians?	Bridal Consultant
7. Who is paying the Officiant? Do they have the money/check/card?	Best Man

scheduled to begin in twenty minutes. Finally, someone came up with the idea of sticking knives into the ground through the holes in the wicker to anchor them and, gladly, it worked.

Sometimes, it is challenging to balance the influence and agendas of the different people helping you design your wedding day. For example, many couples get involved with the caterer in planning the timing of the different food and beverage events. Often, either swept up in the excitement or without thinking of the implications, they agree to serving alcohol to the Wedding Party before the ceremony, along with having an open bar or cocktail hour for guests. This may sound like a really good idea to the facility or caterers, and it may be what they are used to doing. But, from a religious or spiritual point of view, alcohol before the ceremony violates the sacred nature of the ceremony. It is so easy to get caught up in the spirit of celebration and be unwittingly influenced by the marketing hype about having a drink to calm your nerves that the deeply solemn or sacred nature of the ceremony itself gets lost in the shuffle.

Even for a seemingly simple wedding celebration, once a couple has taken the time to determine their own preferences, it is important to assemble a good support team and to communicate, negotiate, and delegate. Couples have their own strengths and weaknesses in this regard, and may or may not have hired professionals to assist them. Therefore, it is essential that they know what needs to be done and who can be counted on to do it.

Usually, if the ceremony is to be held at the same facility as the reception, there will be a Wedding Coordinator for the location. Typically, the Location Coordinator will advise you about where on the property you can hold your ceremony (both indoors and outdoors) and will assist by providing any tables, chairs, sound equipment, or other props that you might need, or will offer suggestions of suppliers in the area. They're also an excellent resource for finding referrals for Officiants, Musicians, Florists, and other service providers. It is important to make sure the Location Coordinator attends your Rehearsal so any last-minute details can be handled. Again, the checklists and worksheets in this book are intended to help you anticipate the decisions that need to be made and the bases that need to be covered.

Some Officiants who see their role solely as that of performing the wedding ceremony do not attend the Rehearsal. Others facilitate the couple's process of identifying and addressing their ceremonial logistics and creating their customized text. Each Officiant has his or her own style, and there are no reliable rules of thumb here. Therefore, again, it is up to each couple to find out how the Officiant perceives his or her role. Many couples hire a Bridal Consultant to coordinate all aspects of their wedding day. This relieves them of enormous pressure and provides the couple with a professional who knows what needs to be done to create a wonderful wedding.

There are no hard and fast rules about who will take charge of what aspects of your ceremony, so pay close attention to the strengths, weaknesses, and points of view of your advisors; use the checklists in this book, and don't be shy about delegating. For example, if you have a passive Officiant and a top-notch Coordinator, by all means ask the Coordinator to take charge. But be sure he or she communicates with the Officiant ahead of time so they can figure out how they want to work together. Ultimately, it is the couple who is in charge and, even if you have a Bridal Consultant, you should never forget that. Above all else, tend to the details ahead of time so you can be as relaxed as possible on your wedding day, and delegate, delegate, delegate.

THE WEDDING PROGRAM

Many couples like to create a wedding program to provide their guests with some basic information about the ceremony. While not a necessity, it can be a nice touch if well designed. Typically, the wedding program lists the order of the ceremonial elements to help guests follow along even though the segments of the ceremony might not actually be identified in the spoken text. Sometimes the text of the readings and lyrics of songs are also included. A list of the ceremony participants helps the guests know who is who. Some couples who have written their own vows like to include them as well. Others like to include a favorite poem, especially if one of them has written a special poem for the other. Finally, some couples like to put in a note of thanks to their parents or other loved ones for their love and support in their lives.

THE WEDDING REHEARSAL

If anyone tells you that you don't need a wedding ceremony rehearsal, consider the possibility that you are being ill-advised! Even if you have the most straightforward and simple ceremony planned, you'd be amazed at all the little details that can be handled at the Rehearsal rather than catching you by surprise in the midst of your actual ceremony. Consider the Wedding Rehearsal Checklist—Sample on the next page and use the blank copy on page 355 to create your own.

One thing to remember about the Rehearsal is that it is the beginning of the actual festivities. People may be arriving from long distances and many will be seeing each other for the first time ever or in a long while. Even if you have provided wonderful directions, inevitably at least one key person will be late. So, you might want to set the Rehearsal time with the Officiant so it actually occurs a half hour after the time you've told everyone else. This allows for the latecomers to arrive and for the reunions that will be occurring to have a little time before the Rehearsal begins, without inconveniencing your Officiant.

What follows is a review of how I conduct a typical Rehearsal. Even if your Rehearsal will be done in a different way, this recap may remind you of some details you'll want to go over. Be sure to

The Wedding Rehearsal Checklist—Sample

Prior to the Rehearsal, contact the Officiant and Location Coordinator to discuss who should attend the Rehearsal, who will be in charge, and what elements need to be rehearsed. List the sequence of Rehearsal events below.

* *Assemble Wedding Party at the altar. Review specifics of positioning the Wedding Party, props, decorations, and chairs.*
* *Rehearse how the Bride and Groom will meet and take their places at the altar.*
* *Have Wedding Party reassemble at starting positions for Processional and rehearse the seating of the mothers and other honored guests and then the Processional itself.*
* *Practice all ceremonial gestures that will involve the Wedding Party moving from their positions, including such activities as the Candle Ceremony and fluffing the bridal train.*
* *Rehearse the Ring Exchange and Wedding Vows.*
* *Rehearse the Recessional, noting exactly where the Wedding Party is recessing to after the ceremony and who will be signing the license and where they will meet the Officiant to do so.*
* *Review with Ushers how to greet and seat the guests.*
* *Encourage and answer any remaining questions.*
* *Remind Wedding Party what time they are expected to be ready on the wedding day and where to meet.*
* *Be clear as to who will be giving any cues needed, for example: starting the Processional, introducing Readers, passing the bridal bouquet, and fluffing the Bride's dress.*

Things I need to bring to my Rehearsal:

* *A copy of the wedding ceremony.*
* *One complete set of all checklists and worksheets, including a diagram of assigned seating for honored guests and ceremony participants, the site layout, and Processional and Recessional Cues Worksheets. Bring enough copies to distribute to all who'll need one.*
* *Bring props to be used during the ceremony, including candles, matches, and a wine glass.*
* *Bring the music tape and equipment. Be sure the person who will be operating it will be there to rehearse and test equipment and ensure that plugs reach outlets.*
* *Bring marriage license and payment to give to the Officiant.*

find out ahead of time who will actually run your Rehearsal and what they'll need from you.

As a rule, I don't go through my portions of the ceremony text during the Rehearsal so it will be fresh and new to everyone at the ceremony. What seems to need the most attention is coordinating everyone for the Processional, Recessional, and where they will be positioned during the ceremony. If you have filled out and brought your checklists and worksheets for the location, Processional, Recessional, and Rehearsal, then the Rehearsal should run very smoothly. Be sure to provide copies of your checklists to the Officiant and Location Coordinator, and bring them to the Rehearsal to let your Wedding Party read through them as well.

I usually begin by positioning the Wedding Party in their places at the altar and then make sure the Bride and Groom like the arrangement. It's important to be specific so that the women don't end up facing forward while the men are at an angle. I also ask the men to decide what they will do with their hands and to all use the same hand positions. Many want to fold their hands in front, not realizing this communicates insecurity in body language. I usually tell them this discreetly and they are more than willing to hold their hands either at their sides or behind their backs. I also remind the Maid of Honor and Best Man that it would look best if they avoid the temptation of reading over my shoulder. It's a natural tendency, and yet they regret having done it when the photos come in. When a ceremony is being videotaped, the Wedding Party is well-advised to keep this in mind, as every gesture they make is likely to be immortalized.

Children who are to be in the ceremony should be instructed at this time about where they go when they reach the end of the aisle— either sitting with a parent or standing with the Wedding Party. I always make it a point to introduce myself to the children and suggest that they may want to focus on me while coming up the aisle. This way they aren't as likely to hang their heads and, if they aren't smiling, I can usually smile at them to remind them.

Once everyone is in place, I ask the couple to go over the placement of all decorations and props such as flowers, tables, and whether or not a podium or microphone is being used for readers. We then review the sequence and cueing of the Processional. Again, if the checklists and worksheets have been filled out, this will be easy. For the mothers of the Bride and Groom and any other guests to be ushered to their seats just before the Processional, it is important to go over which Usher is seating which person and in what sequence. For example, if mothers of the Bride and Groom are to be the last guests seated, the mother of the Groom is seated first and then the mother of the Bride. If grandparents or others are also to be seated, they precede the mothers. The Groom's people are seated first in each category and alternately with the Bride's. Be sure to prepare a list ahead of time of reserved seating for family, readers, soloists, and parents of children in the ceremony. The Bride and Groom should also demonstrate to the Ushers exactly how they want guests to be seated and then practice seating the mothers and any other honored guests.

When that is done, I rehearse with the Bride, her escort, and the Groom how they will meet at the end of the Processional. Typically, the Groom steps forward and paces his steps to meet the Bride and her escort at the front row. When the Groom steps forward, the Best Man and Groomsmen all step over one place so that the Best Man is now standing beside me. The Groom and the Bride's escort greet each other, and then the Bride and her escort kiss or do some other form of parting gesture. The Bride takes the Groom's left arm and they walk forward to their places facing each other in front of me while the escort waits for the Bride's train to pass, then sits down.

If the Bride's gown has a train, then the Maid of Honor usually gives her flowers to one of the Bridesmaids and fluffs the Bride's train when the Bride and Groom arrive at the altar. At this point the Bride may choose to either pass her flowers to her Maid of Honor or continue to hold them for a portion of the ceremony—usually until the Candle Ceremony, Wedding Vows, or Ring Exchange. The Bride and Groom may choose to join hands, depending on the level of formality of the ceremony. It never hurts to remind the Bride and Groom and Wedding Party that this will be a good time to take a few deep breaths if they are feeling nervous on the actual wedding day.

With everyone standing in their places, and before actually rehearsing the Processional, we make a final review of the sequencing cues, including what music will be playing, the seating of honored guests, the arrival of the Officiant, Groom, and Groomsmen, the sequence of people in the Processional, and, if there is to be an aisle runner, when it will be rolled out and who will do so.

Next, it is time for everyone to take their places, practice the Processional, and rehearse those parts of the ceremony that do not simply involve me reading from the text. Some couples don't want to rehearse their vows so they will be a surprise to everyone on the actual wedding day. If the couple is doing a repeat-after-me type of vow, I ask them to rehearse so we can be sure that I am sizing the phrases in a way that is comfortable for them. I like to rehearse the Ring Exchange as well. The Best Man usually has the rings, even if there is a Ring Bearer with a pillow. Often fake rings are sewn on the pillow. This avoids the possibility of losing one or both of the rings, or any awkwardness involved in getting the rings off the pillow. Whoever has the rings is advised to inconspicuously get them ready while the couple is exchanging their vows. I then ask for the rings with my extended index finger. The Groom's ring is placed on my finger first and then the Bride's ring, as I will be giving her ring to the Groom to present first. When the Bride and Groom are exchanging rings, there is no need to struggle getting the ring over the other person's knuckle. Rather, if the ring does not go smoothly over the knuckle, the one giving the ring should just move the ring as far as it goes gracefully, and then after finishing his or her statement, the receiver will move the ring over his or her knuckle. Again, rubbing hard soap on the inside of the rings will make them go on more easily.

Any logistics of movement, such as the lighting of a Unity Candle also need to be rehearsed. I ask the couple to bring the candles to the Rehearsal so we can practice this and they can get comfortable with the sequencing of their actions with my reading. It also gives them a chance to make sure the candles fit and stand in the holders. Often, it is necessary to get some foil or candle-fitting wax so that the candles will fit snugly. In some cases, candles may need to be trimmed with a knife, so be prepared for that possibility. Also, I always prelight the candles so they will light more easily during the ceremony.

I encourage anyone who will be reading or singing at the ceremony to rehearse. They often resist in embarrassment, but I have found that it usually makes it easier for them to read or sing at the ceremony, having done so at the Rehearsal for a smaller audience. It also provides the opportunity for them to receive feedback regarding their volume and pace. For singers who are not professionals and do not know the acoustics of the particular space in which the ceremony will take place, a Rehearsal is usually welcome.

Finally, the Bride's bouquet should be returned to her, either just before the Final Blessing or after The Kiss and before the Recessional, depending on what is comfortable for the Bride. If no one has questions, I then explain how the Recessional will go and make sure that we review the order in which the honored guests will recess after the Wedding Party. Reviewing the order is especially important if there are both parents and stepparents involved. We also discuss exactly where the Wedding Party will be going once they get past the guests. Sometimes, there will be an immediate receiving line, and other times, the Wedding Party goes off for photographs while the guests go on to a cocktail hour. Once this is clarified, we rehearse the Recessional.

Members of the Wedding Party should pause before walking down the aisle so the Photographer can get a good picture of them. I usually suggest that once the Bride and Groom have passed the last row of guests, the children follow them. Then, the attendants recess as couples, beginning with the Best Man and Maid of Honor, each waiting for the previous couple to pass the last row of guests. After the Wedding Party has recessed, the honored guests will follow. First will be the Bride's parents, then the Groom's parents. Next, the Bride's grandparents, followed by the Groom's grandparents. Depending on the layout of the site, I either recess down the aisle after the grandparents or slip off to the side after the honored guests have recessed.

Having previously asked the couple to bring the marriage license to the Rehearsal, we go over it to make sure everything is in order. This also gives us a chance to discuss how they want to handle signing the license. Some want this photographed and others do not. There are also different styles of licenses, some requiring the Bride and Groom to sign after the ceremony, along with the Officiant and witnesses. Others just require signatures from the Officiant and witnesses. If there is an immediate receiving line, I often exit at the end of the line, have the license signed, and then say good-bye to the couple. If there is not a receiving line, we can usually find a moment to sign the license right after the ceremony.

In order to avoid the awkwardness of seeking payment for my services on the wedding day itself, I arrange ahead of time for the couple to pay me at the Rehearsal. I learned this through experience, having left a number of ceremonies where they forgot to pay me and I had to contact them after their honeymoon to get paid.

A Note about Ushers

If you choose to have Ushers seat your guests, usually Groomsmen double as Ushers, but sometimes family members are asked to greet and seat the guests. Be sure and think through the role of your Ushers as well as specifically how you want your guests seated. Do you want to have separate sides for the guests of the Bride and Groom? If so, do you want the Ushers to ask each guest, when being seated, on which side they should be seated? If not, what do you want the Ushers to do if a guest announces "Bride's side" or "Groom's side" to them? At the Rehearsal, be very specific with your Ushers about what time you want them to begin seating the guests—especially for an outdoor wedding on a hot day. Guests are sometimes reluctant to leave the shade of a nearby tree for the sun for any longer than necessary. If guests are hanging around in the background, the Ushers need to be firm but polite in encouraging them to sit so the ceremony can begin. Also, don't assume that your Ushers know how to usher. They may have been shown a different style of seating guests, or they may be clueless, so save them all the embarrassment of not being sure if they are doing it right. At the Rehearsal, demonstrate exactly how you would like them to greet and seat your guests.

Part Two

Designing Your Ceremony

5

The Ceremony Text

The wedding ritual is the ceremonial container for the celebration of a couple's love and their decision to journey through their lives together. To assist those of you who are embarking on the adventure of designing your own wedding ceremony, this section of the book contains collections of passages for each of the traditional ceremonial components. You are encouraged to trust your own instincts as you read through the choices, selecting those elements that are right for you. The worksheet Designing the Ceremony Text is a tool to help you collect those passages that speak to you as you create a very rough first draft. The sample provided on page 65 is an example of how one couple started the brainstorming process. Read it over, and then begin with the blank form provided for you on page 356. Simply reflect on the passages included here and you will find the ones that speak to you. Like looking in a mirror at your own reflection, certain passages will resonate with your inner truth. Feel free to find sentiments in one section that you would like to use in another, to change or eliminate words or phrases, or to use only a sentence or two from here or there. With the exception of rewriting poetry, give yourself lots of editorial license.

As with any well-constructed ritual, a wedding ceremony has a certain flow and order to it that leads up to the sacred moment of the exchange of Wedding Vows, Ring Exchange, and the Pronouncement that the Bride and Groom are now wife and husband. The format presented in this section provides a sequencing of components that allows for flow and order, yet room to customize the ceremony to your own taste.

It is a good idea to start with a rough draft and allow yourself to explore various ideas without being concerned about what will be in the final version. Like filling your plates at a smorgasbord, just gather all those items that appeal to you—discernment will follow. This relaxed approach fosters creativity and provides opportunity to consider the various components of the ceremony over time. It also allows you to carefully evaluate and negotiate any passages that one of you likes and the other does not.

You may feel a bit overwhelmed by the volume of text choices presented here. However, you are likely to find that the process of elimination goes much faster than anticipated, and that you will be able to come up with a rough draft in several hours. Another approach some couples prefer is to work with each other on only one or two ceremonial elements at a time in a series of shorter meetings. At this point, you may not have chosen readings, and if you are planning to write your own vows, you may want to do so after the first draft is written. Then you can work with the draft, giving careful consideration to specific wording and sequencing, and adding or deleting words and sections until it is just what you want. Whether the Officiant is actively working with you on the ceremony text or you are working on your own, it is a good idea to set specific deadlines for completing the text well in advance of the ceremony. Most of the couples I work with prefer to exchange email drafts until the text is complete.

Since I am the one who does the majority of speaking in a wedding ceremony, I maintain the master copy of the ceremony to be sure I incorporate all changes in the final text. I always give each

Create a rough draft. Use the sample text elements that have been included in this book and any others that you have gathered for inclusion in your ceremony. For example, you may want to include a religious or family tradition. List all items in the order in which you would like them to occur. If you only want a segment of a sample item or want to change the wording, make note of that here as well. Remember, this is just a rough draft. So don't be too concerned about editing at this point. Just focus on gathering those elements that speak to you, at least in part. At this stage, you are likely to select more passages than will appear in your final ceremony text.

Opening Prayer: *#4, page 77*

Gathering Words: *#3, lines 1–12, page 84, #5, page 86*

Remembrances and Acknowledgments: *#3, lines 1–3, page 107*

Names to be included: *maternal grandparents*

Readings and Songs:

Selection: *First Corinthians*

Author:

Reader or Singer's Name: *Nan Evans*

Declaration of Support: *#3, page 118*

Marriage Address: *#2, page 128*

Sacred Rituals: *Candle Ceremony #1, page 138*

Wedding Vows:

Groom: *To be written later*

Bride: *To be written later*

Ring Exchange:

Prelude: *Prelude #8 and #9, pages 197–198*

Ring Exchange: *#1, page 199*

Final Blessing: *#3, page 205*

Benediction:

Other:

Once you have created a rough draft according to your directions above, begin the editing and fine-tuning process. Be sure to read the text aloud to see that it flows smoothly and is not too long or short for what you want. Set a specific deadline for completing the ceremony text well in advance of the ceremony.

couple a copy of this final text as a keepsake or to accommodate guests who want copies of certain passages. Many couples like to keep their ceremony among their wedding day memorabilia. On their anniversary, some rededicate themselves to their vows, perform the Candle Ceremony, or quietly reread their ceremony together. It is a loving reminder of the foundation they have laid for their marriage.

Ceremony Overview

Most wedding ceremonies have a fairly consistent structure. The two primary purposes of this section are to introduce you to this format and share with you a variety of options for each of the various components. Before reviewing the parts of the ceremony and samples of each, let us first review the overall structure of the ceremony. Think of your ceremony as consisting of a beginning, a middle, and an end. The beginning sets the tone and starts the process of aligning everyone present into one accord in support of the Bride and Groom. Remember, while this is your day, it is also a day in the life of all the other people who are participating in or attending your wedding festivities. Arriving at the ceremony, each person is in his or her own world. Some may arrive late, some may get lost en route, someone will probably get a run in her nylons, and most people are emotionally up against their own level of success or failure in the territory of love and commitment in their lives. The opening of your ceremony needs to reach out to everyone and gather them together into as harmonious a group as possible.

Usually, the ceremony begins with a Processional, followed by an Opening Prayer or Gathering Words about the meaning of love and marriage in our lives and the joy of having the couple's families and friends with them on their wedding day. Those who start with an Opening Prayer usually follow it with Gathering Words.

Some couples also choose to include a remembrance of loved ones who were unable to attend.

The middle of the ceremony is where you will have the most opportunity to customize. Many couples like to actively involve the guests in the ceremony. For example, you might want everyone to recite a prayer together. Readings and musical pieces also fit in the middle. If you would like to incorporate a religious or spiritual ritual—such as a Candle, Tree, or Water Ceremony—this can appropriately conclude the middle segment of the wedding ritual. The final sequence of the ceremony consists of the Wedding Vows, Ring Exchange, Final Blessing, Benediction, Pronouncement, The Kiss, and the Recessional. It is a good idea to keep this progression uninterrupted, as it creates a very nice flow and climax to the ceremony.

In the Beginning
The Seating of the Guests

Most couples accommodate out-of-town guests by providing directions and maps to the locations of the wedding ceremony and reception. However, getting from the parking area to the specific site of the wedding ceremony can be a great challenge if proper signage or other assistance is not provided. To save your guests frustration and minimize late arrivals, write out specific instructions for how to get from the parking area to the ceremony; include this information with your invitations, and place signs or balloons to direct guests with ease and grace. If the site requires a hike into the woods or to the top of a mountain, or is on a beach, consider providing assistance for elderly or infirm guests to be transported to the site. You will also want to notify guests ahead of time so they can dress accordingly or wear walking shoes.

When your guests arrive at the site, it is important that there be a sense of order and clarity about what they are to do. For example, if it is a beastly hot day and the chairs are set up in a sunny area, your guests may be reluctant to be seated until the last minute to avoid the heat. Be very clear with the Groomsmen or Ushers ahead of time about exactly what you want them to do. You might want one or two to be strategically placed in order to direct guests to the ceremony site. Or perhaps you would like them to greet your guests and direct them to a table of water or lemonade being served by other Ushers under the shade of a tree. Unless directed otherwise, some guests may go in search of the bar to have a drink before the ceremony. Be sure to think about this possibility ahead of time. Do you want your guests consuming alcohol just before and possibly during your ceremony? If the ceremony is about to begin and they have drinks in their hands, it is not uncommon for them to carry them to the ceremony. While this might be unimaginable in a church setting, in an outdoor wedding where the bar is open, it is sure to happen. If it is important to you to preserve a sense of the sacredness of your ceremony, you might want to instruct the Location Coordinator that you do not want any alcohol served before the ceremony.

The first two things that will communicate the tone of your ceremony to your guests will be the visual impact of the ceremony site and the music that is playing. Be sure to use the Ceremony Site Layout Worksheet on page 352 to clarify exactly how you want the site to look and how you want to position the guests, Wedding Party, flowers, Musicians, readers, and so on. The layout is typically much more straightforward in an indoor than an outdoor ceremony. If a Location Coordinator or Bridal Consultant is available, his or her experience with previous weddings can make planning the layout much easier for you.

Remember, if your ceremony starts late, so does your reception, and in most cases that means your reception may be shorter, as the site is typically booked for a specific block of time. Since you are paying by the hour and the kitchen is preparing your food for a specified time, it is a smart idea to start on time. Also, starting promptly is a matter of consideration to your guests.

The Processional

Once everyone is ready to begin, a series of cues sets off the proper sequence of events. In a fairly traditional Processional, the mothers of the Bride and Groom are usually waiting in the back, as they are the last guests to be seated. Sometimes there are other honored guests to be specially seated as well. This seating prompts the Officiant, Groom, and Groomsmen to take their places, which in turn alerts the musicians to begin the Processional music. Traditionally, the Bride proceeds up the aisle on her father's arm, preceded by her Flower Girl, Ring Bearer, Maid of Honor, and Bridesmaids. The Officiant, Groom, and Groomsmen await her at the ceremony site. Some couples prefer to have the Groomsmen escort the Bridesmaids in both the Processional and the Recessional. There are several different ways of bringing the Bride and Groom together. For example, the Groom can meet the Bride and her father near the front row and shake the father's hand. The Bride and her father kiss and then she takes the Groom's arm and steps forward before the Officiant. For philosophical or circumstantial reasons, many couples make other choices. For example, if a couple is older or has been living together for a number of years, the Bride may choose to process unescorted, or the couple may come up the aisle together. In some religious traditions, it is customary for both the Bride and Groom to be escorted up the aisle by both their parents. Or, if the Bride's father is deceased, incapacitated, or not present, the Bride may choose to have her mother, brother, or another family member escort her up the aisle.

If the Bride is wearing a veil or gloves, be sure to decide when the veil will be lifted and the gloves removed (unless they are the type with the ring finger that folds back for the placement of the

Bride's wedding band). Traditionally, the father lifts the Bride's veil over her head and kisses her before she takes the Groom's arm.

Some Brides like to walk on an aisle runner, but few know the origin of this custom. In ancient times, evil spirits were believed to lurk beneath the floorboards of the church. The aisle runner (a roll of white fabric) was believed to protect the couple from those spirits. It also symbolizes the Bride's purity. Traditionally, the runner is rolled out just before the Bride processes up the aisle. However, due to the awkwardness of interrupting the Processional, the runner is often rolled out before the entire Wedding Party processes. In an outdoor wedding, it is challenging enough to walk gracefully up the aisle in your gown with everyone staring at you. When you place a runner on grass, the surface is uneven, bumpy, and awkward to walk on. In an effort to maintain your balance, you might have to lift your feet too high to appear poised and charming. Furthermore, a good gust of wind can twist the runner out of place and create an awkward moment. If you do choose to use a runner outdoors, be sure that at least two people are attending to it. As an alternative, flower petals strewn beforehand or by one or more Flower Girls to create a lovely flower path for the Bride can be a nice touch.

I always remind the Wedding Party at the Rehearsal that it is not uncommon to be struck by nerves, even if you are used to this sort of attention being focused on you. In a perfect world, everyone would just smile, breathe, and walk slowly in tempo to the music. However, no matter how many times I remind couples to relax, I still sometimes find myself faced with terrified smiles spanning their faces and obviously no air moving through their bodies. "Breathe," I whisper, which usually brings them present and helps them to settle in. At the Rehearsal, I remind couples that when they arrive at the altar all they have to do is breathe, smile, and emotionally connect with one another. A few really deep breaths while the Officiant begins the ceremony does wonders to settle the nerves.

If there are children in the Wedding Party, take particular care to anticipate their needs. For example, if there is one Flower Girl and she is young and shy, you might want to have one of her parents or a friendly relative waiting for her up near the front. She is likely to be a bit startled when she arrives at the altar area if nobody is there to direct her. A parent can keep her off to the side until the rest of the Wedding Party has arrived, and then send her up to stand with the others. Alternatively, the parent can take her to sit down. It's always a good idea to reserve front-row seats for parents of children in the Wedding Party so the children can sit or stand according to their behavior or comfort level on the day of the wedding. While Rehearsals go a long way to help children prepare for the big day, you can never predict how they will react to all those people staring at them and exclaiming how cute they are. That situation can be intimidating, even for the most poised children.

While children are cute in a Wedding Party, be careful not to overdo it. In one wedding I performed there were about sixteen children. The boys processed first blowing bubbles followed by the girls throwing flower petals from their baskets. A fun idea, but chaotic in the execution. It turned out the boys couldn't walk and blow bubbles at the same time. One would stop to blow a bubble and the others would bump into him. It was quite a miracle that they made it all the way up the aisle.

Remember that kids are people, too, and being in a wedding can be very stressful. Don't assume that every child would love to be in your wedding. Make sure they think it is a good idea too. I remember one little girl who thought she would have to tear the petals off the flowers. She was quite upset about hurting the flowers. We told her that she would have a basket full of just flower petals, but that was still a problem for her because she realized that someone had removed those petals from the flowers. We settled on a basket of artificial flower petals, and she was happy. In another instance, there were four little Flower Girls who were to process in pairs up a very long aisle. One of the first two girls was painfully shy, and while she did fine at the Rehearsal, during the wedding itself she buried her face in the shoulder of her partner and closed her eyes coming up the aisle. How distressing that must have been for her! Some children never make it at all or make spectacles of themselves. If you are going to have children in your ceremony, keep your sense of humor handy.

As the Wedding Party processes up the aisle, there is the question of where they will go. Traditionally, they stand with their backs to the guests, facing the Officiant. I prefer to have the attendants standing beside me facing the guests while the Bride and Groom face each other in front of me. That way, everyone can see more. If there are a lot of attendants, they can stand at an angle rather than facing fully forward, so they are actually facing the Bride and Groom, and can all fit into the photographs more easily.

If the Bride's gown has a train, one of her attendants can fluff it when she first arrives at the altar and again should she move during the ceremony, and finally when she is about to recess. Some Brides like to hold their flowers until the exchange of vows and rings. Others like to have their hands free to hold hands with the Groom, in which case either a table or an attendant should be available to hold the flowers.

The Processional Cues and Sequencing Worksheet—Sample that follows exemplifies how you can detail your preferences for your wedding Processional. You can find the blank copy of this form for you to use on page 357.

Now that we are moving on to the options for your wedding text, please review the sample worksheet on page 65 and prepare to use the blank copy found on page 356. Notice that each ceremony element and sample in this part of the book is assigned a number

Processional Cues and Sequencing Worksheet — Sample

1. Describe what will happen prior to the Wedding Party processing. Include who will determine when to start and who will cue whom; if mothers, grandmothers, or other honored guests will be formally seated; how the music will be coordinated; and how the Officiant, Groom, and Groomsmen will take their places.

- *The Bridal Consultant will let the Groom know when the Wedding Party is in place and ready to process. The Groom will decide when enough guests have arrived to begin the Processional.*
- *The mothers of the Groom and Bride (who have been waiting behind the seated guests) will be escorted to their seats.*
- *Once the mothers are seated, the Officiant, Groom, Best Man, and Groomsmen will take their places at the altar. The Groom will stand to the left of the Officiant with the Best Man to his left and the Groomsmen to the left of the Best Man. They will all stand with their hands behind their backs and at an angle facing where the couple will be standing.*
- *The Musicians will then start the bridal Processional music.*

2. Describe the order in which the Wedding Party will walk up the aisle and where each one will go. If there is an aisle runner, who will attend to it and how will they be cued?

- *First, the two Flower Girls will walk side by side up the aisle. They will be met by their mothers, who will take them to their seats beside their mothers in the front row.*
- *The three Bridesmaids will go next. The first to walk up the aisle is the one who will stand farthest to the right of the Officiant. Markers (placed on the floor at the rehearsal) are on the floor to indicate where each one will stand at an angle facing where the couple will be standing, mirroring the Groomsmen on the other side.*
- *The Maid of Honor goes next and stands to the right of the Officiant.*
- *The runner is rolled out down the aisle by _____ and _____ .*
- *Finally, the Bride and her father (on her right) come up the aisle. When they are about halfway up the aisle, the Groom moves forward to meet them at the first row. When the Groom steps forward, the Best Man and Groomsmen all step one place closer to the Officiant. The Groom and the Bride's father shake hands. The Bride's father lifts her veil and they kiss. The Bride takes the Groom's left arm and they walk forward together to stand facing each other in front of the Officiant. The father waits for them to step past him and then sits down.*

for easy reference. So for the first draft of your own ceremony text, all you need to do is write down the number of the samples you like (in whole or in part) on the worksheet. When you are done with this brainstorming list, you can copy all of the parts together for your second draft, and then work from there. Please note that the underlining of such titles as "Bride" and "Groom" is to alert you to places you will want to insert the names of your ceremonial participants.

You will notice the same or similar sentiments or passages repeated in slightly different contexts. For example, a passage in a prayer, although identical to one found in a selection from the Gathering Words, may sound more sacred when recited as a prayer and more philosophical in the context of the Gathering Words.

Opening Prayer

When I think of the Opening Prayer in a wedding ceremony, I am reminded of a particular picture of Jesus from my childhood in which he is standing at a garden door that has no handle on his side. The image reminds us that the door opens from the inside. Similarly, an Opening Prayer is a way to invite God's presence at your ceremony. For those who do not believe in God or those who want less emphasis on God in their ceremony, a prayer could be written to unite the guests as one in their love for the couple. When an Opening Prayer is fitting, the tone and language of the prayer can express many different sentiments. For example, some may want a universal concept of God invoked, or they may want to omit the word "God" from their prayer.

Opening Prayer #1

Let us begin by welcoming the presence of God
within each of us.

As we lift into the loving
that joins us together as one,
let us surround <u>Bride</u> and <u>Groom</u>
with our love, our prayers,
and our best wishes for them
on this, their wedding day,
and throughout their journey together
as husband and wife.

Another ecumenical prayer could be as follows.

Opening Prayer #2

Beloved God,
we welcome your presence in our hearts today.
We have come together
as a community of family and friends
to witness and bless the vows of <u>Bride</u> and <u>Groom</u>
and the beginning of their journey together
as husband and wife.
We ask that you bless them
with a loving, healthy, and happy marriage.

We also ask for a blessing of renewal,
devotion, kindness, and loving
for each of us present,
that we may demonstrate our love for you
through our love of each other
in all of our partnerships and family relationships.

Others may want to address God directly, declaring their intentions and asking for God's guidance and blessing for the couple, as in the following prayer.

Opening Prayer #3

    Beloved God,
we welcome you
and are so grateful for your presence
here with us today.
We have come here
as a community of family and friends
to love and support <u>Bride</u> and <u>Groom</u>,
to witness their entrance
into the sacred and joyous covenant of marriage,
and to celebrate
the beginning of their journey together
as husband and wife.

We are here because we love <u>Bride</u> and <u>Groom</u>.
We rejoice that they have found each other
and that through each other,
they have come to know the power of love
as they have never known it before.

We celebrate this union
of their hearts, minds, bodies, and souls
and wish them great joy.

We ask, Beloved God,
that you guide and bless <u>Bride</u> and <u>Groom</u>
with a loving, healthy, and happy marriage.
We ask that through this union
they may come to know you more deeply.

A more Christian version of the final portion of this prayer might be as follows.

Opening Prayer #3a

We call forward and stand
in the light of the Holy Spirit
and the light of the Christ within each of us.
We join together
in support of <u>Bride</u> and <u>Groom</u>
and ask, as a community gathered in your name,
Beloved God,
that as you gladdened the wedding in Cana of Galilee
by the presence of your Son,
so, by his presence now,
bring your joy to this wedding
and bless <u>Bride</u> and <u>Groom</u>
with a loving, healthy, and happy marriage.
Amen.

Opening Prayer #4

Let us come into the quiet of prayer.
Beloved and Eternal God,
we are here to celebrate
the marriage of <u>Bride</u> and <u>Groom</u>.
We pray that they each may find a depth of kindness,
caring, and joy through this union
that will serve as a safe haven for them
as they journey through their lives together.

We also pray that together they may build a life
that brings them balance, health, and great learning
as they venture through

the trials and triumphs to come.
May they strengthen their bond of love
and find a gentle peacefulness
in being together hand in hand.

And finally, Beloved,
for those of us who are here with our partners today,
we ask for a blessing of renewal and devotion
to the vows we have made.
May we comfort each other with our love
today and every day.
God bless us all.

Opening Prayer #5

Let us lift our hearts together as one
in jubilant celebration
of the marriage union we are about to witness
between <u>Bride</u> and <u>Groom</u>.

As they enter into
the sacred and joyous covenant of marriage,
we are blessed to witness
the magnificence of their love,
their open hearts,
and their vibrant and willing spirits.

Inspired by their love,
let each of us rededicate ourselves
to the loving relationships in our own lives.
May we all be enriched
for having shared this day together.

Opening Prayer #6

Lord God,
we call forward the presence of the Holy Spirit
and the light of Christ
to fill us, surround us, and lift us
into a communion of loving
as we witness and bless
the marriage of <u>Bride</u> and <u>Groom</u>.

Beloved God,
we honor your presence within each of us.
We know you
through the divine spark of your loving,
your wisdom, and your truth within our hearts,
where you reside in pure and perfect love.

Through our love and with Spirit's blessing
we extend to you
our prayers and best wishes
for <u>Bride</u> and <u>Groom</u>
on this, their wedding day,
and throughout their journey together
as husband and wife.

The following Opening Prayer is from The Book of Common Prayer.

Opening Prayer #7

Dearly beloved,
we have come together
in the presence of God
to witness and bless the joining together
of this man and this woman
in Holy Matrimony.

The bond and covenant of marriage
was established by God in creation,
and our Lord Jesus Christ adorned this manner of life
by his presence and first miracle
at a wedding in Cana of Galilee.
It signifies to us the mystery
of the union between Christ and his Church,
and Holy Scripture commends it
to be honored among all people.

Into this holy union
<u>Bride</u> and <u>Groom</u> now come to be joined.
The union of husband and wife
in heart, body, and mind
is intended by God for their mutual joy;
for the help and comfort given one another
in prosperity and adversity;
and, when it is God's will,
for the procreation of children
and their nurture in the knowledge and love of the Lord.

Therefore marriage is not to be entered into
unadvisedly or lightly,
but reverently, deliberately,
and in accordance with the purposes
for which it was instituted by God.

Opening Prayer #8
Dearest and beloved God,
we pray for <u>Bride</u> and <u>Groom</u>
as they enter into the sacred vows of marriage,
that they may live according to their promises

each to the other
and that they may create a marriage
that is filled with joy and tenderness.
We pray that they may enter into
the deepest mysteries and wonders of love
and therein create
a safe haven in their hearts for each other.
May they know the peace
that comes from truly being received
and known and accepted by another.

May their love for each other
enrich them as individuals
and provide a safe and loving environment
for the family they are creating through this union.

Guide them and bless them, Beloved,
that they may know
that there is nothing more priceless
than the gift of loving one another
as they journey through life side by side.

When a marriage results in the creation of a new family because the spouses have children from previous marriages, some couples like to include or somehow acknowledge the children in the ceremony. The following Opening Prayer is an example of how that can be done.

Opening Prayer #9
Beloved God,
we are gathered here,
uniting our hearts as one
in support and celebration of <u>Bride</u> and <u>Groom</u>

as they enter into
the sacred and joyous covenant of marriage.

We ask you to bless the family created by this union
as <u>Bride</u>'s daughter, <u>Child 1</u>,
and <u>Groom</u>'s son, <u>Child 2</u>,
join with them in the creation of a new family.

We ask that you guide and bless each of them
in loving and honoring one another
and in building and strengthening a family unit
that will be a safe and nurturing haven for them all.
Help them to find the balance and harmony
of their individuality and their shared life.

We ask that your light and grace
be extended to each of them,
that they may know you and welcome you in their lives
each and every day.

Gathering Words

For those of you who do not want to begin your ceremony with an Opening Prayer, the Gathering Words are a good place to start. This section is where the ceremony focuses on such themes as the meaning of love and marriage, and the importance to you of having your families and friends present with you on your wedding day. For those beginning with a prayer, the Gathering Words could follow the prayer. Feel free to mix and match sentiments from among the following examples and to include ideas you have found elsewhere.

The following is an example of how the Gathering Words might be used to begin the wedding ceremony.

Gathering Words #1

Welcome.
A wedding is such a wonderful occasion,
filled with hopes, dreams, and excitement.
We are here today to celebrate the love
that <u>Bride</u> and <u>Groom</u> have for each other,
and to recognize and witness their decision
to journey forward in their lives
as marriage partners.

A more formal and traditional beginning to the Gathering Words might be as follows.

Gathering Words #2

Dearly beloved,
we are gathered here
in the presence of these witnesses,
to join together this man and this woman
in holy matrimony;
which is an honorable estate,
revered since time immemorial
as the most profound and tender of human relationships.

It is therefore not to be entered into
unadvisedly or lightly,
but reverently and deliberately.
Into this holy estate
these two persons come now to be joined.

The following selections are grouped thematically by the meaning of love, marriage, and the gathering of the couple's families and friends. This first group of passages (Gathering Words #3–8) focuses on the value and importance of love in our lives.

Gathering Words #3

For those of us blessed by a true partnership of love,
we feel safe in the presence of our loved one.
There is no need to hide any part of ourselves
for fear of being judged or rejected.
We can just be together from moment to moment,
believing that those moments
will thread together into eternity.

There is a gentleness to the presence of love
that softens life's rough edges.
It makes us somehow braver
to go forth into the world
knowing that the shelter of someone's love
awaits us at day's end.

We are most vulnerable when we love.
We place our trust in another
to honor us and to care for us,
to treasure us and to receive our love.

In love, we trust that the other will provide a safe haven
in which we can experience and share
the fullness of our being with one another.
And in so doing,
we trust that our lives will be far richer
than had we chosen separate journeys through this world.

We trust that our love will fill us full
and make us wiser and more beautiful beings.
We find that our union graces our lives with balance,

a sweetness beyond any we have ever tasted,
and a treasure beyond any measure of value
we have ever known.

Gathering Words #4

Whenever we attend a wedding celebration,
we are given the opportunity
to reexamine our own lives.
We might look at the radiance
of the couple before us
and be tempted to compare their obvious joy
to the quality of our own primary relationships.

The truth is that each one of us
is a powerful creator
in the dance of love and marriage.
Each one of us,
each moment of every day,
has the choice to rededicate ourselves to one another
or to withhold our love and caring.

Love is powerful.
It is simple.
Yet it is very complex.
In order for love to flow between two people,
four things must be happening at once.
Each person gives their love to the other
and each is the receiver of the other's love.
Love requires us to be vulnerable to each other
so that our love may flow back and forth
through these four doors.

There are so many ways that we can choose
to be in relationship to each other.
It is only through love
that our spirits are lifted into a oneness
that transcends all the dualities
we experience in our lives.
Loving is the only experience that enables us to see
that our separation is only a condition
of the physical and material level of being—
that our souls can soar and merge as one.

It is love that gives the deepest meaning to our lives.
It is our highest calling,
our greatest purpose,
and our finest achievement.

Gathering Words #5

If you ask most couples
who have a strong and abiding love
what they like most about their partners,
usually they will say
that they don't have to pretend
to be anything other than what they are.
They are able to express themselves
without fear of being judged or rejected.
There is room in the relationship
for both of them to be unique individuals.
They are free to surrender
to the possibility of profound intimacy—
to be known and loved without condition.

Gathering Words #6

For quite some time now,
<u>Bride</u> and <u>Groom</u> have known and loved each other.
They have been strengthened by their love
and have received many blessings
through its beauty and tenderness.
They have learned that they can depend on each other
and on the power of their love,
and that through each other
they are becoming better people.

Today, they come before us
to enter into the sacred covenant of marriage,
vowing to be partners through the trials and triumphs
of their shared life.
They are declaring to each other
and to all of us present
that they will be by each other's side,
no matter what life brings their way.

Gathering Words #7

Love has gathered us here today.
We are here to celebrate the love
that <u>Bride</u> and <u>Groom</u> have for each other
as well as the love that each of you has given them
throughout their lives.
As families and friends,
you are the ones
who have taught <u>Bride</u> and <u>Groom</u> how to love.
You have shown them the blessings
that come through loving one another.

Having planted this seed of love in them,
we are now gathered to support them
as they embark upon their voyage of discovery
as husband and wife.
We are here to see them off on this journey.
Let us also be there to see them through.

Gathering Words #8

Bride and Groom have been together
for quite some time now.
As the years have gone by,
their love has grown stronger and more beautiful.
They have learned that they can depend on each other
and the comfort of their bond
to bring forward an abundance
of gifts and lessons into their lives.

Through their sacred union in marriage this day,
they are declaring to each other
and to this gathering of their families and friends
that they will be by each other's side,
no matter what life brings their way.

The next passages (Gathering Words #9–13) express the power and importance of marriage. The first is from The Book of Common Prayer.

Gathering Words #9

The union of husband and wife
in heart, body, and mind
is intended by God for their mutual joy;
for the help and comfort given one another
in prosperity and adversity,

and, when it is God's will,
for the procreation of children
and their nurture in the knowledge
and love of the Lord.

Therefore marriage is not to be entered into
unadvisedly or lightly,
but reverently, deliberately,
and in accordance with the purposes
for which it was instituted by God.

Alternatively,

Gathering Words #9a

The commitment of a man and a woman in marriage
is of the heart, body, mind, and spirit,
and is for the intention of mutual love, help, and comfort
through the trials and triumphs of life.
It is a relationship not to be entered into
unadvisedly or lightly,
but deliberately, lovingly, and reverently.

Knowing and embracing this,
<u>Bride</u> and <u>Groom</u> have invited those present
to witness their union.

Gathering Words #10

The marriage relationship provides the opportunity
for the most intimate joining together of two people.
It is multidimensional
as the union occurs in heart, body, mind, and soul.
It is the most enduring and comprehensive relationship
that can be experienced between two individuals.
Therefore, the choice to enter into marriage is profound.

In choosing a lifelong partner,
we are choosing the one
who will witness our changes and growth,
and who will affect these changes
and shape our maturation as well.

On this day, Bride and Groom
are acknowledging their shared values
and are choosing a future with each other,
their destinies colored
by having experienced life together.

Gathering Words #11

We are gathered here together
as family and friends
to celebrate the coming together of Groom and Bride.
We come to witness the joining
of this man and this woman in marriage
and to rejoice in their making
of this important and lasting commitment.

The essence of the marriage relationship
is the openness to another person
in his or her entirety
as lover, companion, and friend.
We join our lives together
in search of something greater and richer;
something that transcends our solitary lives.

Really loving one another with depth and passion
is perhaps the greatest treasure
we human beings can attain.

It adds richness and profound meaning to our lives.
Love is one of life's greatest joys.
By simply giving ourselves to each other,
honestly and courageously,
each partner is infinitely enhanced.

As companions in our day-to-day lives,
we take pleasure in sharing
our time, thoughts, and feelings.
We delight in reporting on
our separate adventures in the world.
These become the rhythm of life
between devoted life partners
as they build their life together.

In marriage, two lives are intimately shared;
and the blending of the two
must not diminish either one.
Rather, it should enhance
the individuality of each partner.

As a marriage matures, it takes on a life of its own.
And within it,
each partner is individually evolving
while growing in understanding of the other.
This wonderful intimacy with another person
can mirror a depth of inner knowing
that awakens levels of awareness
we never knew existed.
To be awakened in this way is a priceless gift.

When we give of ourselves
into a loving marriage partnership,

we do not abandon ourselves;
we do not shed our individuality;
for that is what brought us together in the first place.

Gathering Words #12

The marriage ceremony is a ritual
representing an institution rooted in antiquity.
Marriage serves as the model for all relationships.
In marriage, two people turn to each other,
reaching for a greater fulfillment
than either can imagine achieving alone.

The marriage ceremony is a bold first step
onto the path of your life together
as husband and wife.
Each of you is risking what you are
for the sake of what you yet can be.
Today, through the ritual of marriage,
you are joining together in your entirety
as lovers, companions, and friends.

Remember that this is a sacred union
in which two people join together
in a bond of loyalty, devotion, and freedom,
allowing the eternal dimensions of life
to emerge and be known.

Bride and Groom,
this day not only signifies
a celebration of shared values and commitment,
but it attests to the fact that you have chosen
to build your future together.

Through the sacred vows of marriage
you are saying that who you are
and who you want to be
can best be achieved through this union.

Bride and Groom,
remember that love and faithfulness alone
will provide a solid foundation
for a long and happy marriage.
No relationship is more tender
than that of husband and wife.
And no promises are more sacred
than those of marriage partners.

In keeping faithfully to your vows
and in bringing to this marriage
the best that is within you,
your life together will be filled with grace and joy,
and your home will be a place of peace.

Gathering Words #13

Being married is like trying to keep your balance
in a three-legged race.
You are walking side by side in a forward momentum,
yet each of you is making choices,
moment by moment,
that will either help you maintain balance together
or cause you to lose your rhythm,
your balance, or your way.

While you are two separate individuals,
you walk along one path together.

Your every gesture, word, expression, and action,
and those you withhold or omit,
will determine the quality of your experience together.

It is through loving, kindness, caring, and sharing
that a successful marriage journey is created.
A good marriage takes patience,
dedication, humor, and forgiveness.

You keep your love alive
through the choices you make moment by moment,
day after day, and year after year.
Through practice,
you learn how to love yourselves and each other
with devotion and freedom.

Spiders build webs, birds build nests,
and we build safe and comfortable havens
through our loving.
Bride and Groom,
through your marriage, and through your love,
may you give the gifts of tenderness,
comfort, joy, and peace to each other
to nurture you throughout the years.

The following passages (Gathering Words #14–17) express sentiments regarding the couple's gratitude for having their family and friends with them on their wedding day.

Gathering Words #14

One of the great joys of the wedding day
is the joining together

of the couple's families and friends.
Bride and Groom are filled with gratitude
to each and every one of you
for the loving, caring, friendship, and support
that you have given them throughout their lives.

Being able to share their wedding day with you,
surrounded by your love and support,
is a treasured blessing.
Knowing that your best wishes
go forward with Bride and Groom
strengthens them as they embark upon their journey
as husband and wife.

Gathering Words #15

Bride and Groom have asked all of you
to be with them today
because each of you has given something of yourself
into their lives.
Your friendship and love
will always be appreciated.
They welcome you here
and thank you for sharing
this important day with them.

Gathering Words #16

Bride and Groom are truly blessed
to be surrounded by their dearest family and friends.
They are so grateful to you
for all of the unconditional love,
joy, support, and guidance
you have given them over the years.

They deeply appreciate
having you all here with them today
to share their joy
and to celebrate their marriage.

Gathering Words #17

Bride and Groom have brought us together here
for an occasion of great joy
and a cause for great celebration.
Having found each other,
they have built the kind of relationship
that will serve them well
as the foundation for their marriage.
They have chosen each and every one of us
to be here with them
to witness their Wedding Vows
as they join together as husband and wife.

Each of us knows that a marriage is not created
by a law or a ceremony;
rather it occurs in the hearts of two human beings.
It grows out of loving,
caring, and sharing ourselves with another.
And so it is that Bride and Groom
have connected their hearts and souls,
one to the other,
drawing upon the depths of their being,
into the deep well of human need—
the need to live united, loving, and complete.

The Wedding Ceremony Planner

So, in witnessing this ceremony today,
we are observing only an outward sign of an inward union
that already exists between <u>Bride</u> and <u>Groom</u>.
Today, they have come before us
to publicly affirm their love;
to promise to nurture themselves,
each other, and this union;
and to acknowledge its centrality in their lives.
They do so knowing
that marriage is at once the most tender,
yet challenging, of all relations in life.

And so, we have gathered here together
as family and friends
to witness and to celebrate
the coming together of <u>Bride</u> and <u>Groom</u>
as they enter into
the sacred and joyous covenant of marriage.

Another appropriate theme for the Gathering Words is to offer guests the opportunity to rededicate themselves to their own marriages or primary relationships.

Gathering Words #18

As we rejoice in <u>Bride</u> and <u>Groom</u>'s marriage today,
let us each consecrate the relationships in our own lives
and rededicate ourselves to these unions we share.
Let us each choose the path
of loving and caring for one another
and of making these commitments
a priority in our lives.

A nice ending for the Gathering Words might be as follows.

Gathering Words #19

So let us come together now,
as families and friends,
to witness, to support, and to celebrate
this union of <u>Bride</u> and <u>Groom</u>.
Please join me in wishing them
a healthy, loving, and joyful marriage.

Sometimes, the wedding location bears particular meaning for the couple and they like to share that with their guests in the Gathering Words, as in the following two examples.

Gathering Words #20

We are gathered here in this beautiful place
to witness the joining of <u>Bride</u> and <u>Groom</u> in marriage.
They particularly wanted to invite you here
because their sense of spirituality
and the growth of their love
are connected to this place.
They wanted to share with you
the beauty of these mountains
because this is where they have made their home.

During their seven and a half years together,
they've come here on many mornings like this one,
and walked quietly through the mountain laurel,
listening to the wind in the pines.
Their time spent in nature,
climbing some of the mountains you see before you here,
has been a time of connectedness,

of shared reverence for the world,
and a deepening respect and love for one another.

It is this sense of timelessness and peace
that they wanted to share with you
on this, their wedding day.

As you look out over the mountains,
please take a moment for reflection and quiet prayer
to open your hearts and minds
to the love and togetherness we are here to share
through this ceremony.
You may also want to take a moment
to remember those loved ones who are not with us today.

Gathering Words #21

Dear friends,
we are gathered together for an occasion of great joy.
We are assembled in this beautiful place
to witness the joining of <u>Bride</u> and <u>Groom</u> in marriage.

They wanted to invite you here
to experience a place that has special meaning to them
and has nurtured their love for each other.
Just being here together, listening to the birds
and feeling the wind and breezes,
seeing an occasional deer, fox, or hawk,
has affirmed for them the beauty of the connection
that exists between us all
and the need to fill themselves
with the soft and gentle things of life.

As physicians, <u>Bride</u> and <u>Groom</u>
often get swallowed up
by the fast pace of life, as many of us do.
But here, they come home to that tender place inside
that is nurtured by nature's beauty,
timelessness, and peace.

It was here on this rock ledge
that <u>Bride</u> and <u>Groom</u>
first declared their love for each other.
And it was here that they decided
to share their lives as husband and wife.
So it is only fitting that we are gathered here today.

They've learned here that the process
of falling in love with another person
is a little like the exploration of a wild and lovely place,
and that loving another person
can deepen your sense of connectedness to all of life.
They have found that the intimacy
and the surprises of that experience
are a form of reverence and can be a form of wholeness.

And it is this that they wanted to share with you
on the day of their wedding.

The final two selections of Gathering Words serve as examples of what a couple might do to create an intimate sharing of their story with their guests. In the first case, the couple was interracial and had faced many extra trials and triumphs in their love. The second is a shorter, heartfelt, yet lighthearted story of finding your love in unexpected places.

Gathering Words #22

As an ecumenical minister,
one of my basic beliefs
is in the importance of unconditional loving.
That means that we love others
not because they are handsome or rich
or only do what we like,
but we love them no matter what they say or do.
Our loving is not conditioned
by the other person's behavior,
but rather it pours forward
from a wellspring of loving
that we tap into inside of ourselves.
We choose to love them
through good times and bad—
just the way the classic wedding vows suggest.

Those of us who are fortunate enough
to heal our misconceptions about loving
learn that true and sustainable love
comes forth from within,
rather than in reaction to others.
Ever so rarely,
we meet a person who radiates love,
and we just want to be around them.

Those of us who are most fortunate
are able to express unconditional loving
and find a wonderful partner who can do that also—
that's where the true magic of love comes in.
Today, we all have the privilege
of witnessing and celebrating
the union of two such people.

Bride and Groom have a love story
that is filled with wisdom
and inspiration for us all.
So let me tell you their story.

Once upon a time
there was a little white girl named Bride,
and a little black boy named Groom,
who went to the same school
where her father was the principal.
When they were in fifth grade,
Groom first saw Bride at a softball game,
and he started watching for her everywhere he went.

In sixth grade,
they were in the same class
and Groom knew that this was the girl for him
and that, someday,
they would be boyfriend and girlfriend.
He told his friends this
and they, of course, told him he was crazy.
But Groom wasn't crazy,
and he was very patient.
Bride still didn't realize it,
but Groom was always keeping his eye on her.

They became good friends until the ninth grade
when Bride wrote Groom a letter
to let him know that she wanted to be his girlfriend.
Then, on October 28, 1983,
he asked her out
and she said yes!

There were no games—
they knew that they were boyfriend and girlfriend.
And it didn't take long before they realized
that they wanted to spend
the rest of their lives together.

They simply loved each other,
and shared a powerful commitment to that love
that carried them through
good times and bad times
in a world filled with challenges,
including racial prejudice
and rules about who should be with whom.
But the fact that the chemical composition of their skin tones
was different
mattered to them about as much
as having different blood types and eye colors.

Over the years,
not only did they see
beyond society's barriers and challenges,
they also served as an example to others
who learned through them
how to do that as well.

So why didn't they just get married many years ago?
I wondered. And so I asked.

Bride never thought that Groom would propose
and, while that might not have made sense to others,
it was OK with Bride.
She knew they would always be together
and that was what she wanted most of all.

Meanwhile, <u>Groom</u> knew he had some feelings
he needed to heal within himself
before he could be as secure and confident
as he wanted to be
as a black man entering marriage
with a white woman in this world of ours.
And so, he set about working things through.
And <u>Bride</u> was patient.

Then, on October 22, 2000,
he went out, bought a ring,
and asked her parents' permission.
He got down on his knee
and proposed to <u>Bride</u>,
and she cried and cried and cried...
and of course she said yes.

And so here we are, one year later,
and <u>Bride</u> and <u>Groom</u> are getting married
after an eighteen-year journey
of following their hearts together.
They still get all excited
and filled with butterflies
when they see each other
at the end of the workday,
and they still are best friends.
They have learned to rely on each other
to make themselves stronger and better people.

How blessed we all are
to be here with <u>Bride</u> and <u>Groom</u> today
to celebrate the power of their love
and their union as husband and wife.

This world of ours needs all the love it can get.
So let us learn through <u>Bride</u> and <u>Groom</u>'s example
and let us all do everything we can
to support them in keeping the flame of their love
vibrant and radiant.

Gathering Words #23

As many of you know,
<u>Groom</u> and <u>Bride</u> met at her veterinary office
in Greenville, South Carolina,
three years ago.
<u>Groom</u> had no idea
that a thousand miles from where he grew up
in rural Vermont
amongst the dairy farms,
he would meet a girl
with a cow on her license plate;
a girl that cut her own grass
and drove a stick shift
in a car with no air-conditioning;
a girl that understood about such things
as ice fishing and cross-country skiing.

He enlisted the help of his mom
to find out if <u>Bride</u> was single.
That was something he had never done before.

Some say he poisoned his poor dog
so he could return to the clinic week after week.

And so, they began their relationship as friends.
<u>Bride</u> remembers
dinners out with groups of friends.

<u>Groom</u> always made her feel
like the most important person in the room.

She says sometime
during those months of friendship,
she fell in love.
She isn't sure of the exact moment.
Perhaps it was a picnic in the woods,
a surprise champagne toast
with the purchase of her first car,
or when <u>Groom</u> became an assistant
with a caesarian section on a cow
during a date.

Today, these friends become marriage partners,
and the story continues.

Remembrances and Acknowledgments

There are both silent and verbal ways to remember those dear ones who are unable to be with the couple on their wedding day due to either death or circumstances that prevent them from coming. For example, you might have a long-stemmed rose placed on an empty chair in honor of a deceased parent or grandparent, or you might hand the rose to that relative's living partner after processing up the aisle. Alternatively, the couple might want to silently light candles of remembrance for their loved ones. Essentially, the remembrance provides an opportunity to publicly recognize your loved ones who are not present. It might be done using specific names or a general statement, as the following examples demonstrate.

Remembrances and Acknowledgments #1

At this time,
we would like to honor the memory
of <u>Groom</u>'s paternal grandparents,
_____ and _____,
and <u>Bride</u>'s father _____,
*who, while no longer with us physically,
are carried in our hearts.

   Alternatives:
   a. who are here today in our hearts.
   b. who, while unable to be with us here today,
   are carried in our hearts.

Remembrances and Acknowledgments #2

<u>Bride</u> and <u>Groom</u>
have asked that we take a moment
to honor the memory of those loved ones
who could only be here today in spirit.

Bryce's Dad

Remembrances and Acknowledgments #3

There are many special people
who are unable to be here with us today
for one reason or another.
So let us call them forward in our hearts.

We would especially like to remember
_____ and _____,
who were unable to make the trip,
and <u>Bride</u>'s maternal grandfather,_____,
who has passed away.

We also remember at this time
three people through whom

Bride and Groom witnessed and experienced
inspirational commitment and love:
____, ____, and ____.

We welcome their presence here with us today
and celebrate their places in our lives.

Remembrances and Acknowledgments #4

At this time, Bride and Groom
would like us all to remember with them
a very special person, ____,
a loving wife, mother, and great friend,
who, while unable to be here with us today,
is carried now and forever in our hearts.

Remembrances and Acknowledgments #5

At this time, we would like to remember ____,
of the Seneca Iroquois,
revered father of Bride and Bride's sister,
and grandfather to ____ and ____.
____ was known for his honor,
intelligence, integrity, and native spirituality.
He demonstrated unfaltering dedication
to furthering understanding and appreciation
of the natural world.
His spirit lives on
in all fortunate enough
to have known and loved him,
and is felt here today
at this happy occasion.

We also remember Groom's grandmothers,
____ and ____.

Their very special love, friendship, and support
are priceless gifts that <u>Groom</u> carries with him
every day of his life.

These loved ones are held in our hearts.

*There might also be occasion to acknowledge the coincidence of your wedding day with
an important event in the life of one of your dear ones.*

Remembrances and Acknowledgments #6
At this time,
<u>Bride</u> and <u>Groom</u> would like to make
a special acknowledgment of <u>Groom</u>'s parents,
_____ and _____,
who are celebrating their fortieth wedding anniversary
this very day!

Happy Anniversary to you!

Remembrances and Acknowledgments #7
Today is All Saints' Day.
It is a day when we are to remember and honor
the saints who have gone before us—
those who were officially named as saints
as well as those unofficial saints
of our daily lives.

One of the remarkable things that we learn
when we study the lives of saints
is that they were ordinary people
like you and me.
What set each of them apart
was their coming to know

the presence of God in their lives,
and their choosing to Live In God's Holy Thoughts—
otherwise known as the LIGHT.
They lived their lives
as journeys home to the heart of God.

Isn't it amazing
that each of us has the opportunity
to make that same choice with our life?

Which of us will be remembered and honored
as the saints of our times?

Remembrances and Acknowledgments #8
At this time, <u>Bride</u> and <u>Groom</u>
would like to extend their love and best wishes
to <u>Groom</u>'s sister and brother-in-law,
_____ and _____,
who are home in Santa Barbara
giving birth to their first child.

We send our blessings and best wishes
to them and their new baby.

Remembrances and Acknowledgments #9
Today is special for <u>Bride</u> and <u>Groom</u>
not only because it is their wedding day,
but because it is the seventh anniversary
of the day they met
and the second anniversary
of the day they became engaged.

<u>Bride</u> and <u>Groom</u>,
as you move through the years ahead
as husband and wife,
may you come upon this date,
year after year,
only to find yourselves
more deeply and profoundly loving each other.

IN THE MIDDLE

While the beginning and ending portion of the ceremony tend to follow a fairly standard sequence, the central portion offers lots of opportunities to customize the ceremony. Since none of them are required by law, couples writing their own ceremonies are free to pick and choose the elements that are most meaningful to them. For example, they may want to include one or two readings or songs, or to have everyone recite a prayer together. In a Charge for the Couple, the Officiant speaks to the couple about the seriousness of the decision they are making and often asks them to affirm that they have thoughtfully made their decision to be married. In the Declaration of Support, the guests are reminded of their role as a community of support for the wedding couple. In some cases, they are asked to take a pledge of support. The Marriage Address, or homily, is an opportunity for the Officiant to discuss the importance of marriage. In a small gathering, a Friendship Circle calls the guests together in a circle to offer their thoughts and feelings about the couple coming together in marriage. Among the symbolic rituals that might be included in the wedding ceremony are the Candle, Tree, or Water Ceremonies. Each of these options is discussed in further detail below.

Readings and Songs

If you want to have one or more readings in your ceremony, be careful in your selection of readers and texts. For example, while it can be quite adorable to see a twelve-year-old child read anything, there is much lost in the translation when they are given a reading beyond their understanding. First Corinthians, for instance, is very popular, but when in the hands of a child or an inexperienced orator, it often sounds like a greeting card verse rather than a profound piece of wisdom about the actions and attitudes of love. If someone is going to be uncomfortable reading, it is best not to put them on the spot. Select readers who can be at ease in that role. It will make a world of difference in the delivery, and none of your guests will have to suffer discomfort and embarrassment on the reader's behalf. Also, try not to exceed two (or at most three) readings, as that seems to be the critical point when guests begin to wonder how long the ceremony will last.

You might want to include an introduction of the reader and his or her reading in the Officiant's text. Some couples like to include a statement of the reader's relationship to the Bride and Groom, so the guests know who the reader is and what they will be reading. Then the reader can simply get up and read or begin with a personal comment to the couple. For example, the Officiant might say, "Our first reading will be 'Union' by Kahlil Gibran and will be read by the Bride's sister, Kathy Higgins, the Maid of Honor."

Readings can make quite a significant contribution to the ceremony. They tend to fall into three categories: scriptural, poetry or philosophical writings, or pieces written specifically for the occasion. Some people also choose to use song lyrics as a reading. There are many wonderful anthologies of readings for the wedding ceremony as well as numerous websites with readings. Among the more comprehensive collections I have found are: Eleanor Munro's *Wedding Readings* and *Into the Garden: A Wedding Anthology* by Robert Hass and Stephen Mitchell.

In terms of music, a solo by a wonderful singer can be a beautiful addition to your ceremony. Again, it is important to take care in this area, as it is painful for all involved when someone gets up to sing and is terribly nervous or sings off-key. A well chosen song and singer can touch everyone's heart. I remember one ceremony where the Bride's brother sang "The Lord's Prayer" with such sweetness and power that he took my breath away. In another ceremony, a gospel singer sang "Amazing Grace," and afterward you could hear a pin drop. Some of the more popular solo pieces of music for wedding ceremonies include:

"There is Love" by Noel Stookey

"The Prayer" by Carole Bayer Sager and David Foster

"I Will Be Here" by Steven Curtis Chapman

"Love Will Be Our Home" by Steven Curtis Chapman

"Amazing Grace" by John Newton

"Love of My Life" by Carly Simon

Charge for the Couple

Some ceremonies include a component where the Officiant asks questions of the couple to be sure that they are aware of the nature of the commitment they are making to each other. Here are two examples:

Charge for the Couple #1

Bride and Groom,

you have made

a very serious and important decision

in choosing to marry each other today.

You are entering into a sacred covenant as life partners.

As in tending the flowers in a garden,

the quality of your marriage

will reflect the effort

you put into nurturing this relationship.
You have the opportunity
to go forward from this day
to create a faithful, kind, and tender relationship.

We bless you this day.
It is up to you
to keep the blessings flowing
each and every day of your lives together.

We wish for you
the wisdom, compassion, and constancy
to create a peaceful sanctuary
in which you can both grow in love.

<u>Groom</u>, do you understand
and accept this responsibility,
and do you promise
to do your very best each day
to create a loving, healthy, and happy marriage?

Groom: Yes, I do.

<u>Bride</u>, do you understand
and accept this responsibility,
and do you promise
to do your very best each day
to create a loving, healthy, and happy marriage?

Bride: Yes, I do.

Charge for the Couple #2

Bride and Groom,
by entering into the covenant of marriage today
you are declaring your faith in each other.
You have indeed earned this faith and trust
by creating a sound foundation for this marriage.

Your task now is to build on this solid base.
Imbue your loving partnership
with the caring, trust, vulnerability, and kindness
that are essential to a healthy marriage relationship.

In dedicating yourselves to these values
you will create a marriage that is a source of joy,
in which you may both grow in love
and find fulfillment.

Know that you will be tested
by the routines of daily life,
by chance and circumstance,
and by the full cycle of the seasons of life.

Know that together you must encounter life's sorrow
no less than its sweetness,
its frustration along with its grace and ease,
its disappointments along with its fulfillment.

Enter your marriage
confident in the love and trust
you have already created between you.
As you go forward in your journey together
as husband and wife,

devote yourselves to living
according to the vows you share today.

Keep your love alive
with your openness to each other
and your enthusiasm for each other.
You hold each other's hearts
in the palms of your hands.
Be gentle caregivers, honoring this trust.

Let this be a marriage
that enhances your individuality
and allows you to know
the greatest gift that God has given us—
the ability to love one another and to be loved.

Is it in this spirit
and for this purpose
that you have come here to be joined together?

Bride and Groom: Yes, it is.

The Declaration of Support

This ceremonial component serves two purposes. First, it symbolizes that in joining together this Bride and Groom, their families and friends are also joined together in support of them. Second, it provides the opportunity to have the guests pledge their support of the marriage. Three versions of this section of the ceremony follow. The first two are a general and philosophical call to support.

Declaration of Support #1

Bride and Groom,
today we have come together
to celebrate the love you have found with each other.
By being here with you,
each of us is declaring our support
for your decision to join together in marriage.

(To guests)

As families and friends,
you form the community of support
that surrounds Bride and Groom.
Each of you, by your presence here today,
is being called upon
to uphold them in honoring and loving each other.

Always stand beside them, never between them.
Offer them your love and support,
not your judgment.
Encourage them with your kindness and loving hearts,
and honor this marriage
into which they have come to be joined today.

Declaration of Support #2

We give thanks for the gift of love
and the opportunity to enter into its mystery.

We pray that Bride and Groom
possess the kind of love
that will bring them great delight,
peacefulness, and friendship.

May they find their hearts and souls
growing ever more closely together over the years,
and may the sanctuary
of their love and friendship
nurture each of them
in their own most beautiful and unique expressions.
May their love be strong enough
to survive the tides of life.

May they know God's presence in their lives
through their love for each other
and through our love for them as well.

May all of us here be ready
to offer our support when it is needed,
and may we have the wisdom to know when it is not.
And, above all, may we return to them
the love that they have given us.

In the next version, the parents are called forward to stand behind the Bride and Groom to declare their support for the marriage. This action symbolizes the joining together of the two families. Sometimes, couples like this sentiment but do not have the "perfect" families with both sets of parents still married and/or living. In such cases, other family members may be called forward to represent one's heritage.

Declaration of Support #3

When a man and a woman
come together in marriage,
their families and friends are also joined together
into a larger circle of caring.
From now on,

you will know <u>Bride</u> and <u>Groom</u>
not only as individuals,
but as marriage partners,
and your individual lives will be linked together
as members of this community.

Mr. and Mrs. ____,
would you please come and stand behind <u>Bride</u>?

Mr. and Mrs. ____,
would you please come and stand behind <u>Groom</u>?

Mr. and Mrs. ____,
you stand before us
symbolizing the traditions and family
from which <u>Bride</u> comes.
Do you willingly and gladly support
<u>Bride</u>'s marriage to <u>Groom</u>?

Mr. and Mrs. ____: Yes, we do!

Mr. and Mrs. ____,
you stand before us
symbolizing the traditions and family
from which <u>Groom</u> comes.
Do you willingly and gladly support
<u>Groom</u>'s marriage to <u>Bride</u>?

Mr. and Mrs. ____: Yes, we do!

(Families greet each other and return to their seats.)

The form of this greeting between the families will reflect the level of formality of the ceremony as well as how well-acquainted the two families are with each other. Some choose handshakes, others are huggers. Sometimes the Bride and Groom get involved and other times it is simply the parents or family members greeting each other.

Declaration of Support #4

Today, we form a circle of love
around <u>Bride</u> and <u>Groom</u>
as they enter into marriage.
To last, their marriage must be a consecration
of each to the other,
and of both to the wider community
of which they are a part.

That community starts with each and every one of you,
their loved ones.
Through their act of marriage,
<u>Bride</u> and <u>Groom</u> have gathered you around them
like a comforting blanket,
forming their community of love and support
as they move forward
into a shared life as marriage partners.

Now, let us share in a moment
of silently extending our blessings
to <u>Bride</u> and <u>Groom</u>
for a loving, healthy, and happy marriage.

<u>Bride</u> and <u>Groom</u>, it is very special
that you have chosen to celebrate your marriage union
in the circle of your families.

So, I would like to welcome
each member of your families:

(Family members are each called by name, given a flower by the Bride and Groom, then one by one join into a circle around the Bride and Groom.)

This circle of your family
represents your circle of loving, caring,
friendship, and family support.
These people embody the traditions and values
that have brought you to this point in your lives.

<u>Bride</u> and <u>Groom</u>, at this time,
your parents would like to share
their best wishes with you.

Bride's mother:
    <u>Bride</u>, your father and I
are so happy for you today
and filled with pride and joy that our baby girl
has become such an accomplished and lovely woman.
And, as though that were not enough,
you have found a profound love with <u>Groom</u>
and brought this magnificent young man into our family.

Bride's father:
    <u>Groom</u>, I never imagined there would come a day
when I could sincerely feel
that anyone was wonderful enough for our <u>Bride</u>.
But you have changed all that.
She has chosen wisely,
and we are delighted to have you in our family.

Bride's mother:

>Bride and Groom, we have had the good fortune
>to build and enjoy a secure and nurturing marriage.
>Our greatest wish for you
>is that you too have the good fortune
>to share a healthy and happy marriage,
>and that you continue
>to light up the room for each other
>for the rest of your lives.

Groom's mother:

>My dear son Groom,
>nothing could give your father and me greater pleasure
>than to stand here with you today
>knowing that you have found
>what your generation calls your soul mate.
>I have watched you and Bride really take your time
>in getting to know each other
>and in building a solid foundation
>of love and respect for each other.
>And now,
>as you stand on the threshold of your marriage,
>I can truly say
>we support you both without reservation
>and with great enthusiasm.

Groom's father:

>I remember when Groom was a young boy
>and used to love learning
>all the names of the trees, flowers, and birds.
>Now I listen to the two of you
>share your anecdotes and lessons from nature

and am so pleased for you both
that you share this common bond.
Seeing how much you two
love and understand nature
touches me deeply.
You are a wise and wonderful pair,
and you make us all better people
just by knowing you.
May God bless you always.

Some couples like to have their guests take a pledge of support for their marriage.

Declaration of Support #5

I invite each of you as members of this gathering
to indicate your support for <u>Bride</u> and <u>Groom</u>
by answering "I will"
to the following question:

By God's grace,
will each of you
do everything you can
to uphold and care for these two persons in their marriage?

Guests: I will.

I encourage you as families and friends
to always choose your loving
in your thoughts about
and interactions with <u>Bride</u> and <u>Groom</u>.
Stand beside them, not between them.
Come to them with hearts of peace, not judgment.
Honor them and yourselves as children of God.

Honor their marriage
as a sacred union with God.
Show them your kindness, your support,
and your loving hearts.

Declaration of Support #6

Collectively, you represent
the families, friends, and traditions
that have brought <u>Bride</u> and <u>Groom</u>
to this point in their lives.
Please affirm your support for this marriage
by responding "Yes, I do" to the following question:

As part of the community
that surrounds <u>Bride</u> and <u>Groom</u>,
do you offer your love and support
to strengthen their marriage
and bless this family created by their union?

Guests: Yes, I do!

Declaration of Support #7

<u>Bride</u> and <u>Groom</u>
would like to acknowledge their parents,
whose love, support, and nurturing
are such an essential part
of who they are today.
They thank you for being their first teachers
of the power and possibilities of love.

May you take great pride in the fact
that the seeds of love

you have planted in <u>Bride</u> and <u>Groom</u>
will flourish in the formation
of this new family today.
Let us all remember, today and always,
that there is nothing more important
than loving one another.

Marriage Address

In the Marriage Address, the Officiant speaks to the couple about the role of marriage in their lives. Like a homily, it speaks of marriage in a spiritually uplifting way rather than in the form of doctrinal instructions. This fact is particularly important when the ceremony is ecumenical or interfaith, as it does not frame marriage within the particular beliefs or doctrines of any specific religion. Rather, it focuses upon how the joining of two people into a marriage union affects their spirits—the core of their beings. It speaks of the sacred mystery of two becoming one in spirit—together yet separate, and each profoundly coloring the life of the other through the vulnerability and permeability of love.

The first example below speaks of marriage as the most fundamental unit of society; the joining together in body, mind, and spirit of two individuals to share their life's journey. The second half of this passage can be customized according to the unique qualities and characteristics of the love shared by a particular couple. To determine the qualities of your love that you wish to incorporate in this section, you may want to each answer three questions in writing, which you subsequently share with each other as part of the process of customizing your wedding ceremony. If written in the first person, the answers, when shared, will be a claiming and declaration of your love for each other.

The questions are:

1. What is it that I love about ____?
2. Why am I choosing ____ as my life partner?
3. What specifically do we do in relationship to each other that keeps our love alive?

You might be surprised at how articulate you are in putting your love into words. When couples share their answers to these questions in our design meetings, many are moved to tears. One couple had several legal-size pages each and ended up sobbing on the floor in each other's arms. I use these questions as an opportunity to encourage couples to verbalize their love every chance they get. I don't think anyone can hear a heartfelt "I love you" or "I appreciate you" too often.

Marriage Address #1

Marriage is the essence of human relationships.
It challenges us to be of one accord
without abandoning the truth of our individuality.
It challenges us to not lose ourselves in one another,
but rather to walk side by side
heading in the same direction.

As with all relationships,
marriage is an endless presentation of choices
about how we want to be with one another.
Each choice results in either more unity
or more separation.
Choose into that unity, <u>Bride</u> and <u>Groom</u>,
every chance you get.

Sacrifice your judgments, expectations,
and any other ways
that you have learned to separate yourselves
from each other.

Share the gifts of your friendship, humor,
vulnerability, sensitivity, and kindness.
Be sure to find ways each day
to protect, affirm, and support each other,
and to treasure the balance and shared values
that you have found with each other.

Enjoy the intertwining
of your independence with your intimacy.
I wish you the courage
to keep your loving hearts open to each other
for the rest of your lives.
God bless you.

*The following two paragraphs are an alternative to the first two paragraphs of
Marriage Address #1.*

Marriage Address #1a

Marriage is the essence of human relationships.
It challenges us to be of one accord
without abandoning the truth
of our individuality.
It challenges us to recognize ourselves in one another,
and to admire and respect each other
while walking side by side
heading in the same direction—
sometimes so close together
that there will be only one set of footprints.

As with all relationships,
marriage is an endless presentation of choices
about how we want to be with one another.

Each choice presents an opportunity for more unity.
Choose into that unity, <u>Bride</u> and <u>Groom</u>,
every chance you get.

Marriage Address #2

<u>Bride</u> and <u>Groom</u>,
demonstrate your love for yourselves and each other
through caring and sharing.
Stretch your love large enough
to embrace whatever life brings to you.
Let it fill you, surround you,
comfort and protect you.

Let your hearts be truly safe and at home with each other.
Be generous in expressing your love.
Be open to receive love from each other.
Be flexible and forgiving with each other.
Let your relationship be a catalyst
that transforms you
into the expression of your highest selves.

Remember that your relationship
is alive and ever-changing
and that your love is a miracle,
always inviting you to grow, to learn,
to blossom and to expand.
How you regard each other
and how you behave toward each other
will determine the destiny of your union.
It is your creation together,
your sacred responsibility.

Be kind to your relationship.
Nourish it with tender loving care,
and, above all else,
keep your love alive.
Treat it as the precious blessing it is.

Do not just be married or in love;
but let your marriage be an active process
of loving each other.

The quality of your marriage is up to you.
Both of you as individuals
and together as a couple
will choose what kind of marriage you will create,
promote, and allow
through your thoughts, feelings, and actions each day.

In the hardest of times,
always remember to reach for the Godness
the goodness inside yourselves and each other
to the Oneness of our Lord's most loving message of
"When two or more are gathered in my name,
there I am also."

May you always honor the sanctity of your union
and thus be blessed beyond your wildest dreams.

Marriage Address #3

Bride and Groom,
your marriage will, no doubt,
be filled with surprises.
Some you will welcome,

while others will test the strength and flexibility
of your bond.

Your life together will present many opportunities
to refine and deepen your love
and to explore the profound depths of your being.
May you be compassionate with each other
and nurture yourselves, each other,
and this union with tender loving care.

May your love create a safe haven for you both
on the journey that lays ahead of you.
Lead with your hearts
and take the time to do the simple things
that will nurture your love.

Deeply listen to each other—
to your dreams and to your frustrations.
Be helpmates.
Be playful in finding ways
to give your love anew to each other every day.

Let your love be an inspiration to others
to reach for what is good within us all.
May your love be so abundant
that you have plenty to share with the rest of us as well.

It is your love
that has brought us together here today.
May it grow deeper and sweeter
with each passing year.

Marriage Address #4

A true marriage is the ultimate relationship
because it offers the opportunity of limitless intimacy
between two people.
It is a great and challenging adventure
into the depths and heights of human caring,
affection, trust, and understanding.

For those who take its sacred vows,
their lives are intermingled
as the waters of two streams become one,
flowing together into a mighty river.

A true spiritual marriage
is a journey of transformation
into the profound mysteries of life and creation.
In marriage, two become one,
and that one is far more complex and dynamic
than the simple addition of the two.

In marriage,
we do not give ourselves to another,
but rather surrender into something greater
while maintaining our balance
and well-being as individuals.
Together, we co-create a shared identity we call "we."

A truly sacred marriage union
is a vehicle for self-realization
that allows us to know our true selves
by reflection through our loved one.
Thus, marriage is a divine instrument

through which we come to know God's presence
in each other and in the world around us.

<u>Bride</u> and <u>Groom</u>,
you have come here today
to surrender into the co-creation
of something wholly new and transcendent
your precious, sacred, and unique marriage journey
as husband and wife.
Today, you step into a much fuller experience
and expression of the mysteries and miracles of love.

Your precious, blessed, and sacred union
is lovely in its innocence,
mighty in its strength,
and abundant with possibilities.
It belongs to you both.
Over time you will give it an identity.
We wish for you the wisdom,
strength of character,
and divine creativity
to make this a happy marriage,
a safe harbor,
and a joyful journey to share.

Marriage Address #5

Marriage is a magnificent opportunity
to share one's life with another
and to enjoy the adventures inherent
in this most intimate of human relationships.
Today, we gather here
to rejoice with and for <u>Bride</u> and <u>Groom</u>
as they embark on this voyage of discovery.

Bride and Groom,
from this day forward,
this date, ____,
will always have special meaning for you
as the day you vowed to love and to cherish each other
in all ways, always.

Each year when you come upon your anniversary
I encourage you to rededicate yourselves
to the vows you make here today.
Take stock of where you are in your marriage
and how you are doing as marriage partners.
Express your gratitude to each other
for the ways that you have effectively loved
and supported one another,
and forgive yourselves and each other
for any judgments that have come between you.

Show each other
that you can be trusted and counted on as a comfort
when facing difficult times,
and celebrate abundantly
the successes and joys life brings your way.
Let your love lead the way
and be more important than anything else.
Then, your lives together
will be filled with blessings and joy.

Marriage Address #6

Bride and Groom,
this bond you share is a true miracle
and a blessing from God.
Treasure it and carefully tend it each day.

You breathe life into each other
and provide a safe and sacred harbor
where you are able to shed all of your worldly illusions
while witnessing, receiving, and cherishing
the precious truth of one another.

Generously shower each other
with the gifts of your faith, strength, honesty,
beauty, and complexity.

This Marriage Address is customized to acknowledge the creation of a family with children from previous marriages.

Marriage Address #7
  <u>Bride</u> and <u>Groom</u>,
  you began as best friends,
  and now that friendship has grown
  into a loving and abiding commitment.

  Remember that the strength and power
  of the love you share
  with each other and with your children
  stand upon your health and well-being as individuals.

  Be aware of your needs as individuals
  and lovingly communicate them to each other.
  Teach the other how to love you
  and care for you as well.

  Tenderly nurture your children
  so that they always feel your love
  and know that they are safe and cared for.

Celebrate your love for each other
and for the children
each and every day.
Remember that God's infinite wisdom
brought you together
and will continue to light your path
all the days of your lives.

Share the gifts of your friendship,
your patience, and your tenderness.
Always nurture this partnership
with your incredible ability
to communicate with each other,
and your abiding respect for each other's strength,
wisdom, freedom, and differences.

Continue to bless each other with your eternal honesty
and your delight and gratitude
for the glory of being able to share your destiny.

Remember to let each of your children know every day
how precious they are to you.
Surround each other and your children
with your tender loving care.

I wish you the courage
to keep your loving hearts open to each other
for the rest of your lives.
God bless you.

Symbolic Rituals

There are many symbolic rituals that can be included in the wedding ceremony. Some come from traditions associated with the heritage of the Bride or Groom. A sampling of these are included in the section entitled Incorporating Ethnic Traditions on page 236. Here we will look at the more universally used Unity Candle, Tree Planting, and Water Ceremonies.

CANDLE CEREMONY

The symbolism of two becoming one is often enacted in a Unity Candle Ceremony as two families are merged together through the joining of a man and a woman in marriage. It is typically included in the ceremony either before the Wedding Vows or after the Ring Exchange and before the Pronouncement. Personally, I prefer the flow of the ceremony that is created when the Candle Ceremony precedes the Wedding Vows.

The spirit or soul of a person is often thought of as a light that shines within, reflecting the light of God as the source of all life and breath, or as a spark of the divine residing within the individual. Thus, during the marriage ceremony, there is often a ritual using candles to symbolize the joining of the light of the Bride and Groom into a larger flame that represents their marriage union. Most commonly, two taper candles are used to represent the Bride and Groom as individuals, while a larger center candle represents either God as the source of our individual light, or the new and greater flame of the marriage. Some couples like to have the mothers of the Bride and Groom light additional taper candles representing the light of their families as well. This ritual is typically done before the mothers take their seats, before the bridal procession. Sometimes, five candles are used: two for the mothers, one for the Bride, one for the Groom and one for the marriage. Other times, the mothers light the two candles that will later be used by the Bride and Groom.

There are two schools of thought regarding whether or not the individual candles should be extinguished when the center candle, representing the new marriage, is lit. In most cases, they are left burning to signify that the creation of the marriage does not eliminate the autonomy of the individuals who enter it. Alternatively, if the Bride and Groom's candles are extinguished, it can symbolize either the end of their single lives or the supremacy of their marriage over their individual identities.

In some cases, the couple may alter the meaning of the candles to reflect the fact that they relate to the symbolism of light but may not recognize God as the source of life. If there are children from a previous marriage, they may also be included in the Candle Ceremony. These variations are reflected in the samples that follow.

If you are having a Candle Ceremony in an outdoor wedding, you might want to ask the Officiant to precede it with a reminder to the guests that the candles are symbolic of the light that shines within the Bride and Groom. And there is no need to be concerned if one of the candles won't light or goes out because, while Mother Nature can blow out these candles, she cannot extinguish the light that shines within the Bride and Groom. This comment adds a note of levity to the proceedings and puts superstitious minds at ease.

Prelighting the candles before the ceremony and making sure the wicks are a reasonable length improves the probability that the candles will light and remain lit. Some couples like to use hurricane glass covers to protect the candle flames. It is also a good idea to check the fit of the candles in their respective holders. Sometimes, a little aluminum foil or stick-um will do the trick and prevent floppy candles during the ceremony.

Some couples ask within their families to see if there is a three-candle candelabra among the family heirlooms. Others request one as a wedding gift from a particular family member or friend. Or the couple can shop for one that they know will suit their décor. Some couples take the opportunity to reenact the Candle Ceremony and to rededicate themselves to their vows each year on their anniversary as a way to strengthen and affirm their commitment.

A three-candle arrangement is used in the first four samples of this ritual, which are all derived from a verse written by Rabbi Yisrael Baal Shem Tov (1698–1760), the founding prophet of the Hasidic Jewish tradition. In the first example, the center candle represents God and is lit by the Officiant before the ceremony begins. The two side candles represent the Bride and Groom.

Candle Ceremony #1

From every human being there rises a light
that reaches straight to heaven.
When two souls
who are destined to be together
find each other,
their streams of light flow together,
and a single brighter light
goes forth from their united being.
Human love is not a substitute for divine love—
it is an extension of it.

<u>Bride</u> and <u>Groom</u>,
when you see each other
as the divine and eternal beings that you are,
you will never cease to wonder and glory
in your coming together.

The purpose of human love
is to awaken love for God.

The truth that is continually reborn
is that within each human being
burns the spark of the divine.

When two people love one another
with devotion and freedom,
they kindle the awareness of that spark in each other
as nothing else quite can do.

<u>Bride</u> and <u>Groom</u>,
in committing to one another today,
you kindle one another's divine light
and promise always to do your best
to see that light in one another,
to nurture and tend
that divine flame in your partner
as best you can each day,
especially at the times it may be hardest to do,
and the times your partner may doubt or forget
the existence of that light within him or herself.

<u>Bride</u>, take this candle now,
and light it from the center candle
representing the divine source.
As you do so, symbolically enter the sacred trust
to honor the divine spirit in <u>Groom</u>.

<u>Groom</u>, as you light this candle from the divine source,
symbolically enter the sacred trust
to honor the divine spirit in <u>Bride</u>.

Now, bring your individual flames together,
symbolizing the new and greater flame of your marriage,

remembering that just as this union is made stronger
by your strength as individuals,
so are you as individuals
made stronger by the strength of this union.

And never forget that the light of your union,
while made up of
your unique and individual expressions of light,
is continually sustained and renewed
by your connection to
the eternal and inexhaustible light of God, the Source.

Some couples choose to extend the light to their guests as well. The ushers distribute candles to all the guests as they arrive. After lighting and joining together their own candles, the Bride and Groom turn to the Best Man and Maid of Honor to light their candles. They in turn pass the light to other members of the bridal party and then it is extended through the Bride's and Groom's parents to all the guests. Given the time it takes to do this, however, it is best done only in small gatherings. Some background music works well here. The text for this goes as follows.

Candle Ceremony #1a
Will everyone please stand?

Now, share the blessings of your divine love
by passing the light to your guests,
bringing us all more deeply into one accord
as we stand together in celebration
of your sacred union.

As we pass the light,
let us take a moment to look into the eyes
of the one we are passing the light to.

As you receive the light,
take a moment
to silently extend your own special blessing
to <u>Bride</u> and <u>Groom</u> on their wedding day.

The next version of the Candle Ceremony is an abbreviated rewrite of the first version. This one is designed for those who would like to do a Candle Ceremony without reference to God. Here, the center candle represents the marriage while the other two candles represent the Bride and the Groom. A small votive candle is lit before the ceremony begins and the other candles are lit from it.

Candle Ceremony #2

Every human being possesses a special light
that burns within them.
When two spirits, destined to be together, find each other,
their streams of light flow together,
and a single, brighter light
goes forth from their union.

<u>Bride</u> and <u>Groom</u>,
by committing to one another today,
you kindle the light within each other,
and promise to do your best
to always see that light within one another,
to nurture and tend that flame in your partner
as best you can,
especially in difficult times,
when this may be hardest to do.

<u>Bride</u>, take this candle as a symbol of your spirit;
and <u>Groom</u>, take this candle as a symbol of your spirit.

Now joining your individual flames together,
light the center candle which symbolizes the spirit of your union
and the new and greater flame of your marriage.
As you do so, silently vow to tend the spirit of this union,
and never forget that just as this union is made stronger
by your strength as individuals,
so are you as individuals
made stronger by the strength of this union.

*The next adaptation of the Baal Shem Tov Candle Ceremony is designed to include
young children from previous marriages in the candle lighting. The wording has been
altered to be more meaningful to the children.*

Candle Ceremony #3

God has made each person unique,
and each of us is born with special gifts.
Within each of us there rises a light
that reaches straight to the heavens.
And when two people like <u>Bride</u> and <u>Groom</u> find each other,
their light touches together
and a single brighter light
is created from their being together.

When a family is formed as an extension of this union,
the light gets even brighter
because of the light that flows
from the children as well.

The purpose of human love is to awaken love for life.
Within each person burns the spark of life,
and when people love one another,
they make each other more aware
of that spark within each other.

<u>Bride</u>, <u>Groom</u>, and <u>Child</u>,
take these candles now,
and light them from this center candle
representing the source of life.
As you do so,
symbolically enter the sacred trust
to honor the spirit in one another.

Now, bring your individual flames together,
symbolizing the new and greater flame of your family,
remembering that just as this union is made stronger
by your strength as individuals,
so are you as individuals
made stronger by the strength of this union.

May the light of your family
guide you through your lives.
May it always help you to know
that your life has purpose.
May it also show you that
while there is sadness in life,
there is also great joy and comfort.
May this light help you to see
the wonder of the world around you.
May it remind you to see the light in others
with whom you cross paths.
And may the light that is the love you share
grow brighter with time.

This next version is also designed to include children but preserves the language of the first Candle Ceremony.

Candle Ceremony #4

Child 1 and Child 2,
will you please come and join us?

From every human being there rises a light
that reaches straight to heaven.
And when two souls who are destined to be together
find each other,
their streams of light flow together,
and a single brighter light
goes forth from their united being.

When a family is formed as an extension of this union,
the light is intensified
by the light that flows from the children as well.

Human love is not a substitute for divine love.
It is an extension of it.
And when each of you come to know one another
as the divine and eternal beings that you are,
you will never cease to wonder and glory
in your coming together.

The purpose of human love
is to awaken love for God.
The truth that is continually reborn
is that within each human being
burns the spark of the divine.

When people love one another
with devotion and freedom,
they kindle the awareness

of that spark in each other
as nothing else quite can do.

Bride, Groom, Child 1, and Child 2,
in joining together today,
you kindle one another's divine light
and promise always to do your best
to see that light in each other,
to nurture and tend that divine flame in one another
as best you can each day,
especially at the times it may be hardest to do,
and the times when one of you may doubt or forget
the existence of that light within him or herself.

Take these candles now,
and light them from this center candle
representing the divine source.
As you do so,
symbolically enter the sacred trust
to honor the divine spirit in one another.

Now, bring your individual flames together,
symbolizing the new and greater flame of your family,
remembering that just as this union is made stronger
by your strength as individuals,
so are you as individuals
made stronger by the strength of this union.

And never forget that the light of your union,
while made up of your unique and individual
expressions of light,
is continually sustained and renewed

by your connection to the eternal
and inexhaustible light of God, the Source.

Candle Ceremony #5

The lighting of the Unity Candle is a ritual
symbolizing the union of a man and a woman
as they enter into marriage.
The Unity Candle itself represents
the oneness that is being created
by the joining of their individual lives
into a shared journey.
The individual candles symbolize
the uniqueness of <u>Bride</u> and <u>Groom</u>
as they walk side by side heading in the same direction.
They are separate yet one.

The lighting of the Unity Candle
in the presence of God
symbolizes the great mystery
of the union of two becoming one.
<u>Bride</u> and <u>Groom</u>, always remember
that as you join together in marriage,
you are still two separate beings,
each with your own unique needs, dreams, and desires,
and that in marriage,
you are creating a covenant
of loving, caring, and sharing between you.

Now, <u>Bride</u> and <u>Groom,</u>
as you bring these lights
which symbolize your individual selves
closer and closer together,

your individual flames merge
into the greater light of your union.

As you light the Unity Candle
to symbolize the enduring flame of your marriage,
let us each take a moment
to silently express our prayerful wishes
for your happiness and well-being in this marriage.
And let us remember that
just as <u>Bride</u> and <u>Groom</u> are becoming one,
so are we coming together
into a circle of family and friends
in loving support of this marriage.

<u>Bride</u> and <u>Groom</u>,
tend the light of your loving union
with great devotion and kindness.
May you be blessed with a lifelong partnership
of loving and learning through God's grace.

This next Candle Ceremony uses either five or seven candles to include either the mothers
or all four parents of the Bride and Groom. The mothers or parents come forward and
light their candles from two votive candles that are lit prior to the ceremony. They then
turn to light the candles of the Bride and Groom, who in turn light the Unity Candle.
The text is as follows.

Candle Ceremony #6

Within each human being
burns the spark of the divine light
that illuminates us all.

As <u>Bride and Groom's mothers/parents</u> light their candles,
we are reminded of the faith, wisdom, and love
that have been passed on to <u>Bride</u> and <u>Groom</u>
from the generations before them.
Each generation has passed on their light
through the mystery of two becoming one.
And here again today,
we witness the gathering light
as two families become one.

As they light <u>Bride</u> and <u>Groom</u>'s candles,
they pass their heritage
into this newly forming family
and once again two become one.
And finally,
as <u>Bride</u> and <u>Groom</u> light the Unity Candle,
they are symbolically stepping
onto the shared path of their marriage.
May their love for each other
grow deeper each day.
And may they tend this union well
so they may enjoy the fruits of its harvest—
abiding in peace, joy, and happiness.

This last version occurs after the exchange of rings. The couple steps forward, picking up two candles and lighting a large central candle. The text is as follows:

Candle Ceremony #7

This flame you ignite before us today
is strong and shining brightly.
May you tend it well
so that it may shine throughout your lives.

May the warmth of the love it symbolizes
forever bring you courage, reassurance, and comfort
and fill you both with strength and joy.

TREE PLANTING CEREMONY

If a wedding ceremony is being performed on family property, some couples like the enduring significance of planting a tree as a symbol of the new life they are creating in their marriage. This version of the Tree Planting Ceremony is inspired by the Baal Shem Tov Candle Ceremony.

Tree Planting Ceremony #1

Within each human being there is a spirit,
an immaterial essence unique to each individual.
Some might call this a soul,
others an inner voice,
and yet others may give it no name at all.
Yet, we all recognize
the set of motivating passions,
beliefs, impulses, and heartfelt truths,
which make up the person we know as our true self.

When two people meet and share these true selves freely,
a special union develops.
And when it is two naturally kindred spirits who meet,
they intuitively recognize each other
and their kinship as love.

Bride and Groom,
in committing to one another today,
you give expression to the kinship

that exists between you,
acknowledging the new strength and meaning
it gives your lives.
You promise always to be true to yourselves
and to share your true selves with each other.
You promise also to nurture and tend
the spirit in the other,
especially in difficult times
and times when one of you may forget
the existence of that spirit
within him or herself.

It is with these thoughts
that <u>Bride</u> and <u>Groom</u> plant this seedling
in soil from the land of both of their families.

(<u>Bride</u> and <u>Groom</u> plant their seedling.)

Just as the kinship
between <u>Bride</u> and <u>Groom</u>
needs nurturing,
so does this seedling
which symbolizes the joining of two families
and the start of new life.

WATER CEREMONY

Water Ceremony #1

Many of us have been blessed to notice
that when we share
a true and abiding love with a partner,
even plain water tastes sweet.

Bride and Groom,
share this clear water now
as a symbol of the sweet and precious love you share.

(The Bride and Groom give each other a drink from the same glass.)

As you do so,
remember that just as you are now partaking
of the sweetness and purity
of this fresh and clean water,
you have already been blessed
to partake of the brilliance and magnificence
of the love you share.

By devoting yourselves
to cherishing and nurturing this love,
may your marriage grow sweeter
with each passing year.

IN THE END

The final portion of the ceremony includes the Wedding Vows, Ring Exchange, Final Blessing and Pronouncement, Benediction, The Kiss, and the Recessional. This section is the sacred and joyous climax of the ceremony.

Wedding Vows

It is very easy for most couples to get so caught up in the details of selecting their clothing, planning the music, food, guest list, and so on that they lose sight of the fact that the entire day is really about the moment that they enter into the sacred and joyous covenant of marriage by sharing their vows. Through the speaking of vows, you give verbal expression to your commitment in the presence of witnesses.

Typically, the Wedding Vow is a public promise to love, honor, respect, and comfort your partner. And there are as many ways to do this as there are couples in love. There is a certain issue of balance and appropriateness to be considered in choosing your Wedding Vows. For example, if you are having a large wedding including many guests who are not close friends, you might not want to pour your heart out in an extremely intimate Wedding Vow. Or, if your partner is a man or woman of few words, you may want to avoid a lengthy vow. Couples need to discuss their comfort levels in terms of privacy, intimacy, the length of their vows, and whether or not they are traditional or personally written. The tone is also an important consideration. It can be awkward if one partner's vow is rather philosophical and formal and the other's is like a Hallmark card.

Writing your own Wedding Vows can be a beautiful gift from the heart to each other. Some Brides and Grooms are concerned that they will be unable to express themselves well, not realizing or trusting the eloquence with which the sincerity and purity of love can speak through us. When you take the time to write your own vows, it gives you the opportunity not only to personalize them, but to deeply embrace each word you select. The Wedding Vow is not simply pretty words; it is a sacred declaration of commitment about how the individuals intend to nurture, support, and love each other as marriage partners. It is important that the vow be carefully chosen so that it really matches the heartfelt intentions of each partner. Remember that in your hearts and souls you will hold each other accountable for the vows you make to each other. Ideally, you will make beautiful promises to each other, keep your word, and reap the benefits of a healthy and happy marriage.

It is not necessary for both the Bride and the Groom to say the same words. Some even choose to keep their vows secret from each other until their wedding day. While most couples choose to use their first name only during the Wedding Vows, some like to use their full names.

Since the sharing of vows is the foundation upon which the wedding celebration and marriage rest, it is important to find the words that truly resonate with the love and caring you share. While many want to write their own vows, others are more comfortable with traditional vows. In either case, the Wedding Vows can be shared directly between the Bride and Groom or in a repeat-after-me format with the Officiant. Some people find the repeat-after-me format to be distracting and impersonal for this most important moment of the ceremony. I have also noticed that when using the repeat-after-me format, the Bride and Groom often look at me rather than at each other when speaking and tend to focus more on getting the words right than on the love and commitment they are sharing with their partner.

When sharing Wedding Vows directly, there are several things you can do to support yourselves just in case you get nervous. First of all, you can arrange with the Officiant ahead of time to prompt you only as needed. Secondly, you can write your vows on index cards, beautiful paper, or a scroll, which the Groom can have in his chest pocket (over his heart) until they are needed (or they can be held by the Officiant). The Groom gets the vows from his pocket and takes the Bride's hands, holding the cards between them. If the Bride has been holding her flowers up to this point in the ceremony, she will now hand them to the Maid of Honor. The Groom says his vow first, and then the Bride says hers.

Since your vows are really what your entire wedding day is about, you will probably want to be well prepared so you can gracefully and lovingly share them with your beloved. Here are some keys to help you in doing that.

1. Several weeks before the wedding, make up the actual cards you will use during the ceremony and use them to practice. This way, you will be visually familiar with exactly where every word is on the cards.

2. Write or type your vows in verse—not paragraph—format leaving space between each thought. Arranging the information in this way makes it much easier to visually access during the ceremony as needed.

3. Practice your vows daily. Some people find it especially useful to practice in front of a mirror, making eye contact with themselves. Don't wait until the last minute. Remember, these are words of promise to your partner. Give them the gift of your time, attention, and caring, in order to deliver these words meaningfully.

4. Set the intention to know your vows and to be able to share them during the ceremony while looking deeply into your partner's eyes, referencing the card as little as possible. Remember, the point is to share your love, and that is far more important than getting every word just right.

5. Breathe and take your time. It is not uncommon to be nervous or even to cry. Do what professional actors do and breathe deeply to relax and center yourself. And don't be afraid to take as much time as you need for nervousness, emotions, tears, or whatever comes up for you. Some people do everything they can to avoid crying. But consider the fact that your tears tell your partner how much you care and, in reality, fighting them back will make saying your vows more difficult than if you let them flow. Tears are a natural release. I remember one Groom who was so overcome with joy that when he looked into his partner's eyes to share his vow, he began to sob and couldn't speak. She held him and he whispered the beginning of his vow to her until he gained his composure; it was a deeply touching moment for us all. I

encourage you to give yourselves the gift of allowing your exchange of vows to be a sacred and loving foundation for your marriage.

If you choose to write your own vows, or would like to piece together excerpts from the following selection of traditional and personal vows, consider going into your heart to find the themes and dreams you have for your marriage. Don't worry about writing beautiful vows on the first try. Just excavate your heart and soul for what this commitment means to you and what you are choosing to do and be in this marriage. You may be surprised to find within yourself the exact words and phrases that capture what you want to say to your beloved partner in the sacred sharing of vows. If not, there are lots of examples available in the following pages to mirror your inner sentiments for you.

Some couples like to combine the Wedding Vows and Ring Exchange by adding a line to their vows such as "With this ring, I thee wed" or "I give you this ring as a symbol of my promise." However, unless the vows are very easy to remember or are being shared in a repeat-after-me fashion, it can be clumsy to manage the vow cards and rings. If you plan to combine the rings and vows, be sure to rehearse the logistics so it can be done gracefully during your ceremony.

Traditionally, the Groom goes first in both the exchange of vows and the giving of rings. Since the sample vows are interchangeable between the Bride and Groom, I have not labeled the blanks in the text samples that follow.

As with any collection of vows, you will find a great deal of repetition of popular themes here. Still, each vow has its own tone and message. Some of the vows included consist of a pairing of vows between a specific couple. The first sample vow comes from *The Book of Common Prayer* and is probably the most familiar, except for the last line. The next three versions are those traditionally used in the United Methodist, American Lutheran, and United Church of Canada wedding ceremonies.

Wedding Vows #1

I, _____, take thee, _____,
to be my wedded wife/husband,
to have and to hold,
from this day forward,
for better, for worse,
for richer, for poorer,
in sickness and in health,
to love and to cherish,
till death us do part,
according to God's holy ordinance;
and thereto I pledge thee my faith.

Wedding Vows #2

In the name of God,
I, _____, take you, _____,
to be my wife/husband,
to have and to hold,
from this day forward,
for better, for worse,
for richer, for poorer,
in sickness and in health,
to love and to cherish,
until we are parted by death.
This is my solemn vow.

Wedding Vows #3

I take you, _____,
to be my wife/husband,
from this day forward,
to join with you
and share all that is to come.

I promise to be faithful to you
until death parts us.

Wedding Vows #4
_____, I take you to be my wife/husband,
to laugh with you in joy,
to grieve with you in sorrow,
to grow with you in love,
serving mankind in peace and hope,
as long as we both shall live.

Wedding Vows #5
I, _____, choose you, _____,
in the presence of our friends and families,
to be my wife/husband and partner
from this time forward;
to love you,
to be a comfort and safe haven in your life,
to hold you close,
to listen deeply when you speak,
to nourish you with my gentleness,
to uphold you with my strength,
to weigh the effects of the words I speak
and the things I do,
to never take you for granted,
and to always give thanks
for your presence in my life.

Wedding Vows #6
Dearest _____,
I choose you to be my wife/husband,

to be by each other's side
through our life's journey together.

You are my best friend.
You are my precious love.
You are the one I choose to spend my life with.

I promise to cherish you,
to honor you,
to love and respect you.
I promise to comfort and encourage you,
when we are healthy
and when we must endure sickness;
when we are filled with the joys of success
and when we are burdened with sorrows.

_____, I promise to love you without condition
for all the days of my life.

Wedding Vows #7

I, _____, choose you, _____,
as my wife/husband.
I will love you tenderly,
I will laugh with you and cry with you
through the trials and triumphs to come.

_____, I stand before our families and friends
as your lifelong partner.

Wedding Vows #8

I, _____, choose you, _____,
as my life partner.
I am so glad that I waited

for my dreams to come true
by finding you.
I am so blessed that I get to be your partner
and am comforted to know
that I have chosen wisely.

Whatever life has in store for us,
I will honor and respect our marriage
and be by your side,
loving you through it all.
I will always strive to be
the wife/husband of your dreams.
____, I will love you forever.

Wedding Vows #9

As your wife/husband,
I am blessed to receive your love,
I will honor you with my caring,
sensitivity, strength, and gentleness.
I will be kind and honest, fair and true.
May God always keep us
and watch over our love and our home.

Wedding Vows #10

____, each of us has had quite a journey
in our lives so far.
I feel so blessed
to have found you as my partner.

I love you,
and I am choosing to share all of life's blessings,
challenges, joys, and sorrows with you.
As your husband/wife,

I promise to nurture you,
to be kind and patient,
forgiving and faithful.
I promise to honor our differences
and to learn from them.
I will encourage you and stand by you
in our life together,
and will grow with you
in the shelter of our love.

I promise you this with my heart and soul.
I vow to you
before our families and friends,
to dedicate myself to our marriage,
our friendship, and our love.

Wedding Vows #11

_____, I love you
and choose to share my life with you.
I will laugh with you in times of joy
and comfort you in times of sorrow.
I will be at your side
through all of life's challenges.

_____, I will love you forever.

Wedding Vows #12

_____, I promise to love you,
to cherish you,
and to respect you
in all ways, always.

I promise to participate fully
in our marriage partnership.
I will give fully
of my mind, body, heart, and soul.

I promise to make your plans and dreams
as important to me as my own.
I promise to do my share
so that our lives together
can be healthy, happy, and abundantly satisfying.

I promise to lovingly fulfill these vows
each and every day
for all of my days.

Wedding Vows #13

I, _____, promise
to always keep my love for you alive
and out in front of all I do.
I promise to be faithful and true
no matter what challenges may come our way.
I promise to nurture you as my wife/husband,
my lover, and my best friend.
I will continue to love you and cherish you,
walking through this life, together, hand in hand.

*Some couples choose to exchange vows by responding to a question posed by the
Officiant, as in the following two examples:*

Wedding Vows #14

Do you, _____,
of your own free will and consent,

choose ____
to be your beloved wife/husband,
and do you promise
to love, honor, and cherish her/him always?

Groom/Bride: I do.

Wedding Vows #15

____, do you take this woman/man
as your wife/husband and equal,
your lover and your best friend;
keeping yourself only unto her/him,
for as long as you both shall live?

Groom/Bride: Yes, I do.

Wedding Vows #16

I, ____, take you, ____,
to be my wife/husband,
my lover, and my best friend.
I am choosing to share with you
all of life's blessings:
the joys and sorrows,
the successes and disappointments.

____, I will love you and cherish you always.
I promise you this with my heart and soul
for all the days of my life.

Wedding Vows #17

I, ____, receive you, ____,
as my wife/husband.

May we love one another with constancy,
live joyously, laugh freely,
and support our marriage
through the trials and triumphs to come.

I will strive to be fair and honest,
wise and true.
Join me in making our hopes and dreams come true
today and forever.

Wedding Vows #18

_____, the moment I first met you,
I knew deep within my heart
that I loved you.

Now that our love has stood the test of time,
I know that I want to spend my life with you.

I honor you, _____.
I cherish your spirit
and am so grateful
for all the ways you share your beautiful love with me
each and every day.

I will always be true to you, _____,
while remaining true to myself.
I will nurture you with tender loving care
and always be by your side
whenever you need or want me.

I am so blessed,
knowing that I get to spend my life with you

singing, dancing, laughing, and crying.
And that we will raise a family together
with all the joy, passion, gratitude, and love
that we are so fortunate to share.

Wedding Vows #19
I, _____, welcome you, _____,
as my partner in life.

May our love forever nourish us
and keep us strong.

Wedding Vows #20
I choose you, _____,
to be my lifelong partner,
lover, and best friend.
I will always be faithful to you,
and be at your side
to laugh with you in times of joy
and comfort you in times of sorrow.
Wherever our path leads us,
it takes us together.

I will encourage and support you,
honor and love you.
I will respect our differences
and do my part to work through
all our challenges.

_____, I'll be your safe haven and your home.
With purity of heart and love in my soul,
I stand before our loved ones
as your lifelong partner.

Wedding Vows #21

_____, when I look at you,
I see everything that I want and need in my life.
I feel so blessed
every day I wake up and find you next to me.
My love for you is so overwhelming
that at times it leaves me breathless.

After all these years,
I still get excited
to hear your voice on the phone
or to see you after being apart.

My heart aches when we are separated,
yet it is filled with anxiousness to see you again.
I feel butterflies when you hold my hand
and melt when I look in your eyes.
I am so at peace because I have you.

You are my best friend
who has been with me through it all.
You help me feel safe when I am scared.
You help me laugh when I am sad.
You comfort me when I am hurting.
You reassure me when I am doubting.
When you hold me, I feel that everything is possible,
and that no matter what happens,
we can make it through together.

These past _____ years with you
have been so wonderful.
The bond we have built between us is so strong,

I know that nothing can weaken it.
For all that you have done for me and given to me over the years,
I promise to do the same for you.

All I ask of you is to have faith in us
and let the love we share continue to surround you.
____, as I stand here before you
readying to be your husband/wife,
know this:
you have my heart
and I will be yours and stand by you through eternity.
You are my love.

I love you.

Wedding Vows #22

I have known you
since the beginning of time, ____,
and loved you longer still.
I am so happy, so blessed,
that I found you here in this life.

I promise you
that I will never take this great love for granted;
I will always nurture our love
and be awed by its power.

I vow to you that every day,
I will hold this marriage sacred,
for you are the greatest gift of my life.

Wedding Vows #23

____, when I was a little boy/girl,
I used to dream of my Cinderella/Prince Charming.
Then as I grew up and gained some life experience,
I gathered the wisdom and knowledge
of the qualities and characteristics
that would be important for me to find
in my life partner.

In finding you, ____,
my dreams have come true.
In your love, I have found a home
for my heart and soul.

____, I love that I can trust you and depend on you.
I love your sensibility, integrity,
humor, and generosity.
I love all the ways you let me know
how much you love and value me.

____, I honor and respect you,
and consider it a great privilege
to be able to share our lives together.

I, ____, take you, ____,
to be my wife/husband.
May our love forever nourish us
and keep us strong.

Wedding Vows #24

_____, you will always be surrounded by my love.
From this day forward, I promise:
    to be by your side,
    to be your partner, your husband/wife,
    and your very best friend.

Let my love comfort you always.

Wedding Vows #25

In the name of God,
and in the presence of our families and friends,
I, _____, choose you, _____,
to be my beloved wife/husband.

I promise to love you and hold you close,
and to be a comfort
and a safe haven for you in your life.

I promise to nourish you
with my gentleness and caring
and to uphold you with my strength.

I will listen to you with an open mind and heart
and will weigh the effects of the words I speak
and the things I do.

_____, I will forever thank God
for your presence in my life
and you will always be surrounded by my love.

Wedding Vows #26

I, ____, choose you, ____,
to be my wife/husband.
From this day forward,
I promise to love you,
to honor you,
to respect you,
and to support you,
as long as we both shall live.

Wedding Vows #27

____, in the presence of our friends and family,
I offer myself to you in my entirety,
and I accept and love you
without condition.

I promise to support you when you need help.
I promise to turn to you when I need help.
I promise to hold you when you are sad.
I promise to smile with you when you are happy.

My love for you reaches higher than the mountains
and deeper than the sea.
____, I choose to share
the rest of my life with you.

Wedding Vows #28

____, I choose you
for the way your smile lifts my spirit,
for the way you support and respect me,
and for the way you make me feel about us.

I promise to share with you
all my hopes, fears, and dreams.
I promise to nurture your spirit
as I nurture my own.
I will keep laughing with you,
learning with you,
and growing with you.
I will faithfully care for you
with an open heart and with tenderness.

I promise to be there for you,
to warm your toes through the coldest nights.
I promise to remind you how great you are,
just as I did on our first date.

I promise to be at your side in sorrow and in joy
and to love and cherish you always.
I promise you this from my heart
and with my soul
as I dedicate myself to our marriage,
our friendship, and our life together.

Wedding Vows #29

I love you, _____,
and in that love,
and with my deepest gratitude for your presence in my life,
I am honored to become your husband/wife today.

I know that our life together
will include sadness as well as joy.
But I also know
that going through life with you

will make it all more meaningful,
because with you,
I get to live life in Technicolor.

I know that between the two of us,
we have all the resources, imagination,
strength, and clarity of intention
to protect, grow, and nurture our love
through all of life's ups and downs.

____, I promise to respect you always
and to recognize that your interests, desires, and needs
are as important as mine.
I also know
that the quality of our inner life together
is far more important
than anything we can create
or accomplish in the outer world.

I promise to keep my mind, heart,
and soul open to you.
I promise to be vulnerable enough to let you in
to the tender and secret places within me.

____, I promise to love you without condition
with all that I am and all that I have,
completely and forever.

Wedding Vows #30
My dear and precious ____,
on this, our wedding day,
before God and our families and friends,

I declare my intention to love you well
and to love you always, in all ways.

When we are old and sitting in our rocking chairs
looking back on our life together,
I want us to be proud of ourselves
for how well we loved,
honored, and respected each other.
I want us to be full of memories
about how we enjoyed ourselves and each other,
and how we weathered the storms that came our way.
I want us to be joyful, satisfied, and enriched
by the life we led together.

With that vision in mind, dear ____,
I promise not to take you, your love,
or our relationship for granted.
I promise to give my best to you
and to the family we will create together.

I, ____, take you, ____,
to be my beloved wife/husband
for the rest of my life.

This is a pairing of vows between a Groom and a Bride.

Wedding Vows #31
Groom:
> Bride, each of us has traveled a long way
> to be here today,
> and I feel truly blessed to have found you.

Bride, to you I vow these things:
never to forget the wonder of having found you,
never to lose sight of the rare gift
that is your love,
never to take that love for granted,
and always to place our relationship first.

I vow always to be open with my heart,
to be honest, sincere, respectful, and kind.
In the presence of these witnesses,
I take you as my wife and partner,
from this day forward,
in happiness and in sorrow,
in sickness and in health,
in good times and in bad,
in weakness and in strength.

All that I am, I give to you
in a bond that is everlasting.
I pledge my love forever.

Bride:

Groom, I too feel truly blessed to have found you.
My days with you fill me with wonder.
At times you are a mirror to my soul.
Other times you are my perfect complement.
You enrich my life
in ways you cannot imagine,
and with each day you give my life new meaning.

You are my lover, my partner, and my best friend.
As your wife, I will be faithful to you always,

laugh freely with you in times of joy,
and cry with you in times of sorrow.
Whatever path life lays before us,
it takes us together.

I will always accept you for who you are,
wholly and without reservation.
And I ask you to accept me as I am.

Your love is my greatest treasure.
I am blessed by the love,
patience, and devotion you have shown me.

All that I am, I give to you
in a bond that is everlasting.
I pledge my love forever.

Wedding Vows #32

____, you reached out to me
and re-opened my heart
when I had closed myself to the idea of love.
You have taught me to believe in my ability
to love and be loved.
You have enriched me beyond measure.

____, you have restored my faith and enthusiasm
about being in a relationship with someone
as my partner, my friend,
my confidante, my lover, and my soul mate.
I thank you, ____,
from the bottom of my heart and the depths of my being.
As we stand here today,

I am excited about our journey together as marriage partners.
I promise to always be by your side
through the joys and sorrows that lie ahead.
And I promise to keep my heart open to you
for the rest of my life.

_____, I am truly blessed to stand before you as your husband/wife.
With all that I am and all that I have,
I will love you each and every day to come.

Wedding Vows #33

My dear and precious, strong and tender _____,
receiving your love and giving my love to you
is what I treasure above all else in this world.

I promise you that I will pay attention
to the needs of our love
and continue to place it above all else.

You can count on me,
as I know I can depend on you,
to share life's joys and sorrows,
to keep my mind, heart, and soul open to you,
to be honest and true.

And just in case you have been wondering
why those two rocking chairs are over there,
they are my gift to us.
They are the rocking chairs
that will sit on our front porch
in every house we own.
They are the very chairs that we will sit in

when we are old and gray,
looking back on all the years that now stand before us.
I promise to be right by your side, ____, through it all.

I love you today.
I will love you even more tomorrow.
I will love you always.

Wedding Vows #34

____, you are my friend and my partner.
I want to spend all my days, weeks,
months, and years with you,
facing life's worst
and celebrating life's best together.

I am so grateful to you
for all the ways that you enrich my life
and inspire me to stand tall in my truth.
I have known since the moment we met
that you are my greatest blessing.

____, I promise to love you,
comfort you, support you,
and be by your side
building a healthy and happy marriage
and family together.

I, ____, take you, ____,
to be my wife/husband.

Wedding Vows #35

_____, I choose you
to be my lifelong partner.
I offer myself completely to you
and promise to be faithful and at your side,
honoring and loving you
each and every day,
now and forever,
wherever our life may lead us.

Wedding Vows #36

_____, I am honored to stand before you today
surrounded by our families and friends
as we embark upon our journey together as husband and wife.

As your life partner in marriage,
I promise to respect you as your own person
with interests, desires, and needs as important as my own.
I promise to do my part
to weather whatever storms lie ahead
and to joyously celebrate our triumphs.

My intention is to be a wonderful husband/wife to you
and to contribute daily
to the health, balance, and comfort
of our relationship
and the family we plan to create together.

I promise to keep myself open to you,
and to always take delight
in having the privilege of sharing my life with you.

I promise to love you, _____,
in the only way I know how—
completely, and forever.

Wedding Vows #37

_____, it is you, above all others,
who has awakened my soul
and enthused me with the possibility
of becoming all that I am capable of being in this world.
I am so grateful to you for these blessings.

I want you to know
how much I cherish your friendship
and how much I appreciate your belief in me.
Your love is my greatest treasure.

I will be at your side
through all of life's challenges and joys
as we become one in spirit before God.
I promise to give of myself to you
in every way I can,
and to care for you and protect you
as I would my own self.
I promise to be faithful to you in this life,
and to be honest and true to our union until God,
in his perfect wisdom and timing,
calls one of us to Death.

_____, I promise to carry
the flame of your love with me forever
in this world and the next,
so that the light of our love,

now one light drawn
from the mingling of two souls,
will always prevail.

In this next example, the Bride and Groom first speak separate vows and then a final statement of commitment together.

Wedding Vows #38
Bride:

> Your tenderness and love
> have awakened the very best of my spirit.
> With you, I enter life stronger
> and with greater joy.
>
> On this, our wedding day,
> I continue and strengthen my commitment to you:
> to hold your trust tenderly and faithfully,
> to celebrate loudly,
> and to comfort you with my love.
>
> I promise you, <u>Groom</u>,
> to keep my heart open,
> for now and always.
> I will be your home.

Groom:

> I enter this day with you, my love,
> as my soul partner.
> And I ask you to become my wife
> so that our journey through life
> will be forever filled with this balance.

It is only from knowing
your brilliant love for me
that I can finally see my future.
I want to visit each new moment together;
to rejoice, console, and live with you.
Know that I will be forever true to you
and the family we create.

We shall always be my priority.

Bride and Groom:
I am your partner in and for life.

The following Wedding Vows incorporate the Ring Exchange at the end.

Wedding Vows #39
Groom:
Much time and effort has brought us here today.
When I first felt the power of our love,
I couldn't keep from smiling,
like an explorer overjoyed at having reached his destination.

Your love for me was unmistakable,
quiet as a whisper,
strong as thunder.

We both know that we have found a miracle
and that our love will continue to grow
as we experience life together.

From this day forward,
I take you to be my wife,
promising to stand by you,
through all God has in store for us,
faithfully and compassionately,
as long as we both shall live.

Bride, I give you this ring as a symbol of my promise.

Bride:
Groom, I am honored to become your wife,
and feel blessed to have you as my husband.

I promise you today, Groom,
that I will keep an open mind,
a loving heart, and a giving spirit,
and will do all I can
to make our marriage and our family a work of art
to be both treasured and respected.

I vow to cherish you above all others,
and to respect our individuality.

I promise to encourage you
and to support your decisions.

I will laugh with you in times of joy,
and cry with you in times of sorrow.

I promise to always be true.

I will hold these promises close to my heart
and always protect our sacred bond of marriage.
As we stand before our families and friends,
I pledge this vow to you.

Groom, I give you this ring
as a symbol of my promise.

These next vows were shared by a couple who were forming a new family with their five young children from previous marriages.

Wedding Vows #40
Groom:
Bride, I have never before known
the desire and passion
you have created in me.
I never imagined these feelings
were even possible.
Words cannot describe
our spiritual, physical, and emotional connection.
Life is a series of events and experiences
that together make us who we are;
that person someone else sees when they meet you.

Bride, from the moment we met,
I discovered a unique bond
with a truly special person.
My life was forever changed,
and now, with you in my life,
each day is truly lovely.

We came together from separate paths
and today begin our journey
along the same road,
our destinies forever linked,
our lives intertwined.

I have heard that love consists
not of gazing into each other's eyes,
but of looking outward together
in the same direction.

From deep within my heart, I love you.
<u>Bride</u>, in you I have found someone
to share not only the good times, but the bad;
not only the pleasure, but the pain;
someone to support and be supported by.
You are my companion to confide in and console.
You are my best friend.

I am confident that with you,
none of life's obstacles will stand in our way
and together we will enjoy all that life has to offer.

<u>Bride</u>, my love, my soul mate, my partner, my best friend,
today, I ask you to be my wife and companion.
I commit myself to you
for the rest of our lives together and beyond.
Please share with me the joy of guiding my boys,
<u>Child 1</u>, <u>Child 2</u>, and <u>Child 3</u>,
as I will enjoy guiding <u>Child 4</u> and <u>Child 5</u>,
together raising our family.

Who knows what other beautiful facets
our relationship will foster?
For there awaits us all
the pleasure of growing together
in a life shared for years to come.

Bride:
Our love developed over time,
with respect for each other's talent and ability,
into a friendship.

As we supported and guided each other,
you patiently and tenderly broke down my walls.
While you taught me to look into my heart and soul,
we shared our dreams, hopes, fears, and desires.

Sometime, probably sooner than either of us knew,
we fell in love.
I asked you to catch me while I was falling,
and you wrapped your loving arms around me.
Groom, as I gaze into your beautiful green eyes,
I look into your soul and I join you there.

I have fallen in love with you, my best friend,
a thousand times.
I will fall in love with you thousands more,
giving my love to you freely.

Groom, I know that we will be tested
by the routines of daily life,
by chance and circumstance,
and by the full cycle of the seasons of life.

I am entering into our marriage
knowing that together we will face life's sorrow
no less than its sweetness,
its frustration along with its grace and ease,
its disappointments along with its fulfillment.

I promise that, as your partner,
I will do my best to help us keep our hearts open to each other
and the love flowing between us
even at the times this may be hardest to do.

I will remain at your side,
holding you close and supporting you above all.

The strength of the connection we have between us
was evident when we first met.
In our lives, I will continue to explore
and develop that connection.
As I give myself to you in marriage,
I vow to be a loving woman,
filled with passion and friendship,
to make a happy home
for both of us and our children.

When we are apart,
I will always look at the sky and the moon,
knowing that we are together,
never truly apart,
for our hearts and souls
are so incredibly linked.

You have freed my wings for flying,
and I will fly with you forever.

I will look for your secret places
and share mine with you,
always working to keep our love new,
exciting, adventurous, and young,
especially as it grows in maturity and familiarity.

You were made to love me
and I was made to love you.
Our destinies intertwined,
bringing us together here today
and for the rest of our lives.
Keep your loving arms around me.
Our love proves to me that fairy tales really do come true.
It will last forever.

We have reached our island! Love . . .
We are there!

Sometimes, knowing the life circumstances of a couple makes vows that they have written deeply meaningful. For example, this set of vows was exchanged by a beautiful couple—well-heeled, well-spoken, well-dressed—and one would assume they were sitting on top of the world in love. Yet, they were both HIV-positive and had met in a recovery program for intravenous drug users. They were thus facing a very uncertain future. There were no dry eyes in the room as they shared these heartfelt vows.

Wedding Vows #41
Groom:
> <u>Bride</u>, as my heart and soul yearn for your love,
> above all others,
> I ask you to be my wife;
> to join me in living our lives together
> with serenity, courage, and wisdom.

Come with me and we'll grow together,
nourishing the seeds of Love, Faith, and Hope
planted in us by our God.

I promise to love you, <u>Bride</u>,
for who you are,
to honor you as my equal,
to cherish you above all others,
and to respect your individuality.

I promise to encourage and support your decisions
whether I understand them or not.
I will laugh with you in times of joy,
and cry with you in sorrow;
I will be at your side during life's challenges.
I will be gentle and forgiving.
I will be fair and always strive to be honest and true.

As I stand before family and friends,
I pledge this, my vow to you,
and ask you to be my wife.

Bride:
 <u>Groom</u>, I strongly believe that our union is God's will.
 Therefore, through his grace,
 I, <u>Bride</u>, take you, <u>Groom</u>, to be my beloved husband.

 With all the sincerity in my heart,
 I promise to love you dearly,
 to confide in you honestly,
 to respect you proudly,
 and to always be kind.

I have learned, through you,
the importance of being true to myself,
and as your partner,
I will strive to be fair and true to you.

I look forward to our life together,
enriched by our friendship
and the encouragement we give to one another.
And I am comforted to know
you have promised to be by my side
in times of fear and sorrow.

<u>Groom</u>, from this moment forward,
I offer to you all that I am
and all that I hope to be.
I will be faithful to you
and grateful to God for our love
all the days of my life.

Wedding Vows #42

Groom:

<u>Bride</u>, my love,
it is with deep admiration and quiet humility
that I come before you today
to pledge my life to you and to us.
It is with great honor and the utmost respect
that I ask you to be my wife.
And it is with the deepest sincerity
that I vow to be your husband.

You have shown me a beauty
I thought existed only in dreams,
and a love I thought had been reserved for fairy tales.

The Wedding Ceremony Planner

It is with warm fondness
that I look back on our time together,
and with excited anticipation
that I look to our future.
From every meal shared
to every dream realized,
I promise to hold our love and our togetherness
with the highest reverence
and the greatest admiration.

From this day forward,
we shall walk together into our future;
even as we walk separately into our own.
I promise to walk before you when you need me,
behind you when you don't,
and beside you always.

I promise to cherish you and to love you
for all time and beyond.
For our love is, and shall be, immeasurable;
not even the hands of time
shall fashion a boundary on our love.

Bride:
  Groom, our life together
  continues from this day,
  for countless days.
  And so, in the presence
  of our closest friends and families,
  I offer this vow and prayer for our love:

  May I always let my candle light my way
  into your soul

so that I may know your needs
and anticipate your sadness.

May I always be able to ease your fears,
satiate your hunger,
and honor the magic
of your presence on this earth.

May our journey together always bring us more joy
than could the sum of our journeys
on separate paths.

With each sunrise may we dance,
and with each sunset may we happily remember.
May we forever know
our own beauty and strength
because we are so deeply cherished by one another.

On sleepless nights,
let my heart sing you a lullaby.
When you lose your way, let me rekindle your torch.

When we are apart,
may I always feel you running through me
like a river that carries my boat to a safe harbor.

When we are too weak in our journey,
may we carry each other in our arms.
And when we can walk forward no further,
may we return in kind to the earth
whispering in the winds of change.

The Wedding Ceremony Planner

Groom, as your life partner,
I promise to love you
with honesty, dedication, and respect.
I will forever cherish and honor you as I do now,
in sickness and in health,
for richer or for poorer,
for every day you live within me.

Wedding Vows #43

Groom:

Bride, I love you more than everything.
We have been through so much already.
With you at my side,
I look forward to whatever may lie ahead.

You are beautiful and smart, strong yet gentle.
You are charming and fun, intelligent and loving.
You make me laugh at times when I am ready to cry.
You make me smile and relax
even when I am stressed.
You make me a better person just by being in my life.

I love the way you burst into song
and dance for no particular reason.
I love the way you can ignore the rest of the world
and all of its conventions.
I love the way you fall asleep on my shoulder
while trying to stay awake
just so we can spend more time together.

When we are apart,
I am always thinking about you.

I no longer find it sensible to make any plans
that don't include you.
When we are at home,
I don't like us to be in separate rooms.
As we sit side by side,
I love holding your hand in mine.

I vow to always be here for you
and to make any of your problems my own.
I vow to help you with tough decisions
and to always speak my feelings.
I vow to support our dreams
and to shelter you when times are troubled.
I vow to apologize when I am wrong
and to forgive when we misunderstand.
I vow to trust you
and to always believe in you.
I vow to faithfully love you forever
with all of my heart.

<u>Bride</u>, spend your life with me and my life is yours.

Bride:
I love you, <u>Groom</u>, with all my heart.
I have known for many years
that you are part of me
and that we will share our lives together.
With you, I have discovered what love truly means.
I feel lucky for every moment we have together.

You are sweet, brilliant, and fun.
You are extremely gentle and strong at the same time.

You are silly.
You are so logical and level-headed,
yet can be just as nutty as me.
I smile every time I think of you.

I love that you have high ideals
and are not afraid to go after your dreams.
I love that you appreciate the little beauties of life
and live each day to the fullest.
I love that I still get a tingling feeling inside
every time I come home to you.

I vow to always come home to you,
and to always be there
for you to come home to.
I vow always to try to make you laugh,
and to be by your side
when you need someone to hold you.
I vow always to love you for who you are
and to accept the changes that life brings.

<u>Groom</u>, I adore you,
and will tenderly care for you
for all the days of my life.

Ring Exchange

The vows are typically followed by the Ring Exchange—similar to how a signature seals a contract. Some couples do incorporate the Ring Exchange in their Wedding Vows, ending with a phrase such as "I give you this ring as a symbol of my promise." When the exchange of rings follows the vows, this portion of the ceremony generally consists of two parts. The first is a Prelude by the Officiant addressing the symbolic significance of the Ring Exchange. Then comes the actual exchange of rings by the couple.

It's a good idea to rub some hard soap on the inside of the rings before the ceremony so they will go on more easily. Most people are eating richer foods than usual in the prewedding festivities and typically have slightly swollen fingers. At one ceremony, just before taking our places, I checked with the Best Man to be sure he had soaped the rings. Having just flown in from Hong Kong, he was not terribly alert. He responded with surprise and dashed into the men's room with the rings. During the ceremony when I asked him for the rings, he handed me a puddle of slimy soft soap with the rings in it! So remember, hard soap.

PRELUDE BY THE OFFICIANT

Here are some samples of Preludes to the Ring Exchange. Some couples like to mix and match the sentiments.

Prelude #1

These rings are symbols of the love
that joins you spirit to spirit.
They represent the oneness, eternity, and renewal
inherent in the marriage union.

May these rings serve you
and those who see them upon your fingers

don't like any of these but about the rings something

as reminders of the vows you have made here today
and of our need to be faithful in all our relationships.

Prelude #2

These rings are circles,
and circles are symbolic
of the sun, the earth, and the universe.

As arms that embrace,
these wedding rings you give and receive this day
reflect the circle of shared love
into which you enter as partners in life.

May you always be blessed,
and may you abide in peace and love.

Prelude #3

Wedding rings are symbolic reminders
of the unbroken circle of a healthy and abiding love.
Within the safety and comfort of a true marriage,
love freely given has no beginning and no end.
Love freely given has no separate giver and receiver.
Each of you gives your love to the other
and each of you receives love from the other.
And the circle of love goes around and around.

May these rings serve to remind you
of the freedom and the power of your love.

Prelude #4

Bless, O Lord, the giving and receiving of these rings.
May <u>Bride</u> and <u>Groom</u> abide in thy peace

and grow in their knowledge of your presence
through their loving union.

May the seamless circle of these rings
become the symbol of their endless love
and serve to remind them of the covenant
they have entered into today
to be faithful, loving, and kind to each other.

Beloved God,
may they abide in your grace
and be forever true to this union.
Amen.

Prelude #5

Let us pray.
Bless, O Lord, the giving of these rings,
that they who wear them
may abide in thy peace
and continue in thy favor;
through Jesus Christ our Lord.
Amen.

Prelude #6

Rings are adornments,
carefully chosen for their beauty and simplicity.
They quietly sit upon our fingers,
reminding us of the power of love
and the pledge of the wearer to his or her partner
to be faithful and true,
and to nurture their love so it will last a lifetime.

Bride and Groom,
may these rings be for you always
your most treasured adornment,
and may the love they symbolize
be your most treasured possession.

Prelude #7

Just as we bear witness to a written covenant
with our signature,
so, too, do we exchange wedding rings
to seal the vows of marriage.

Wedding rings are an enduring symbol
that remind us of the pledges we have made to each other
and of our responsibility to honor each other
by honoring our promises.

Prelude #8

Bride and Groom,
these wedding rings symbolize
the holiness, perfection, and peace
that is available to you in your marriage.
They are symbols of the love, friendship, and faithfulness
that you share.

As circles, they have no beginning or end.
They are round like the sun, moon, earth, and universe.

Just as these rings have no points of weakness,
may your union be strong,
and may you be blessed with joy
as you journey through life together
surrounded by the circle of your love.

Prelude #9

Wedding rings are a symbol
that has been carried forward from antiquity.
They are simple and strong.
They are round like the sun and the moon,
like the eye, and like the embrace of love.

As circles, wedding rings remind us
that as we give our love,
so it comes back around to us,
and that we give and receive love around and around
in the circle of love.

May your wedding rings always serve as a reminder to you
that your love, like the sun and moon, illumines;
like the eye, lets you see clearly;
and like an embrace, is a grace upon this world.

Prelude #10

The wedding ring is a circle
symbolizing the sun, and the earth, and the universe.
It is a symbol of wholeness, perfection, and peace.

As you enter into the circle of your shared love,
may you be blessed through your devotion to this union.
May your journey as husband and wife
be filled with peace, love, and joy.

RING EXCHANGE BY THE COUPLE

The actual exchange of rings by the couple is typically accompanied
by a statement of the symbolic meaning of the rings or a simple
statement pledging one's love to their partner.

Ring Exchange #1

While exquisitely simple, this first exchange symbolically emphasizes the conscious choice to give and receive one another's love. It draws attention to the fact that, for love to exist between two people, four things must be happening. Each partner must give their love to the other and receive the other's love. In this Ring Exchange, the couple looks into each other's eyes while the Groom places the ring up to the knuckle of the Bride's ring finger and makes a statement such as "I love you." Next, she moves it over the knuckle and responds "I wed you." Then, they reverse roles and the Bride becomes the giver and the Groom the receiver. Alternative responses include:

Giver: "May this ring encircle your finger
               as my love does your heart."
Receiver: "I love you."

Giver: "I give you this ring as a symbol of my love."
Receiver: "I receive your love as my greatest treasure."

Giver: "I give you my love."
Receiver: "I will treasure your love always."

Ring Exchange #2

_____, I give you this ring
in token and pledge of my abiding love for you.

_____, with this ring, I thee wed,
in the name of the Father, and the Son,
and the Holy Spirit.
Amen.

Ring Exchange #3

With this ring,
I give you my promise to honor you,
to be faithful to you,
and to share my love and my life with you
in all ways, always.

Ring Exchange #4

_____, I give you this ring
as a symbol of my love for you,
and of my promise to honor you,
comfort you,
and be faithful to you and to our marriage
through God's grace
for as long as we both shall live.

Ring Exchange #5

_____, I give you this ring
as a symbol of my love and devotion,
in the name of the Father, and of the Son,
and of the Holy Spirit.
Amen.

Ring Exchange #6

As a sign of my love
and my knowledge that in marrying you,
I am becoming much more than I am,
I give you this ring
with the promise that I will love you
and keep my heart open to you
all the days of my life.

Ring Exchange #7

_____, with this ring
I am giving you my promise
to always love you, cherish you,
honor you, and comfort you.
I will always be grateful to God
for your presence in my life.

Ring Exchange #8

_____, from the moment we met,
I knew I wanted to spend my life with you.
With this ring,
I pledge myself to you,
to our marriage,
and to our everlasting love.

Ring Exchange #9

This ring is my gift to you.
May it always remind you
that from this day forward,
you will be surrounded by my love. — *change this last bit!*

Ring Exchange #10

I give you this ring
as a sign that I choose you
to be my lover, my partner,
and my best friend
today, tomorrow, and always.

Ring Exchange # 11

With this ring, I thee wed.

Ring Exchange #12

____, I give you this ring
as a symbol of my vow.
May it encircle your finger always,
as my love will your heart.

Ring Exchange #13

____, this ring is a symbol
of the strength and beauty of our love.
May it belong to your hand
as my heart belongs to you,
separate yet close,
simple yet miraculous.

Ring Exchange #14

I give you this ring
as a symbol of my promise
to always love you, cherish you, honor you, and respect you.

And finally, here is a more traditional version where the Officiant asks the Groom and then the Bride to pledge their love to each other.

Ring Exchange #15

Officiant:

____, do you take ____
to be your lawfully wedded wife/husband,
to love and to cherish
from this day forward?

Groom/Bride: I do.

(The Officiant hands them the rings to place on their partner's finger.)

Final Blessing and Pronouncement

As an Officiant, I always experience a moment of awe when pronouncing couples to be married, and like to imagine that they will all go on to create happy and fulfilling marriages. The Final Blessing gives the Officiant the opportunity to bless the couple and extend best wishes to them.

There are several subtle, but significant, considerations to make in the wording of the Final Blessing and Pronouncement. For example, some couples like to add a touch of formality in both the Opening Prayer and Final Blessing by being referred to with their full names. Similarly, when inviting the couple to share their first kiss as husband and wife, there are various ways that couples like to be addressed. When the Bride is changing her last name, they often choose to be referred to as "Mr. and Mrs. ____" for the first time. Others prefer the informality of being called by their first names. Some Grooms want to hear the words "You may now kiss your Bride."

Other significant variations are the inclusion or exclusion of language referring to God and the subtle difference between being referred to as "man and wife," which suggests that she is his possession, or "husband and wife," which refers to them as equal partners.

Some couples like to include the Apache Wedding Blessing in this first selection.

Final Blessing #1

<u>Bride</u> and <u>Groom</u>,
you have declared your intention and vows
before God and this gathering of your families and friends.

May the grace of this day
carry forward with you all the days of your lives.
May you find delight in each other
and may your love continue to grow
and to nurture you throughout your lives.

I wish you the strength to be true to the vows
you have made here today.
May you always have the wisdom
to cherish the precious love you share.
May you abide by the laws of Spirit
nurturing yourselves and this marriage
with acceptance, understanding, cooperation, and loving.

May the life you share
be peaceful, healthy,
and filled with blessings and joy.

As the Apache Wedding Blessing declares:

"Now you will feel no rain,
for each of you will be shelter to the other;
Now you will feel no cold,
for each of you will be warmth to the other;
Now there will be no loneliness,
for each of you will be companion to the other.
Now you are two persons,
but there is one life before you.
Go now to your dwelling place
to enter into the days of your togetherness,
And may your days be good and long upon the earth."

And now, by the power vested in me by the State of ____,
I witness and affirm your union of love
and now pronounce you husband and wife.

You may now kiss as husband and wife for the first time.
Congratulations and God bless you!

Final Blessing #2

Beloved Father, Mother, God,
we ask you to bless <u>Bride</u> and <u>Groom</u>
with the strength to keep the vows they have made,
and to cherish the love they share,
that they may be faithful and devoted to each other.

Help them to support each other
with patience, understanding, and honesty.
Enable them to have a home
that is a place of blessings and of peace.

We seek your love and grace
for all who are witnesses of this holy marriage.
May all who share the marriage covenant
be renewed through their witnessing this union.

<u>Bride</u> and <u>Groom</u>,
may your life together be joyful;
may you both be enriched and made better people
for living in this blessed union.
May the grace and wisdom of God be always with you.
May the love of God always fill you, surround you, and protect you.
Amen.

Now, go forth in peace, joy, and celebration.

Final Blessing #3

<u>Bride</u> and <u>Groom</u>,
on behalf of your loved ones
who are here with you today,
I would like to mention some of the things
we wish for you:

First, we wish for you a love
that is rich, deep, and powerful enough
to inspire others and to support you both
in bringing forth the best that is within you.
May you lavishly love one another
and love being loved by one another
today, tomorrow, and always.

Second, we wish for you the kind of home
that will be a sanctuary for you both,
a place of peace, freedom, vitality, growth, and humor.
And in this home,
we hope that you are blessed
with a healthy and happy family.

Finally, we wish that at the end of your lives
you will be able to look back
and smile upon the life that you have shared together,
pleased, satisfied, and fulfilled beyond your wildest dreams.

And now, by the power vested in me by the State of _____,
it is my great pleasure to pronounce you husband and wife.

Mr. and Mrs. _____,
you may now kiss as husband and wife for the first time.
Congratulations and God bless you!

Final Blessing #4

Bride and Groom,
our best wishes go forward from this day with you.
We wish for you a fulfilling life,
rich in caring and in happiness.

We wish for you a gentle and peaceful life
that nurtures and comforts you.
We wish for you a noble life,
which reflects your honesty, kindness, and integrit
We wish for you an adventuresome life,
exploring the fullness of your own and each other's ___ selves.

Bride and Groom,
there is a wonderful life ahead of you.
Live it fully.
Love its changes and choices.
Let life amaze you and bring you great joy.

And now, by the power vested in me by the _____ church
and by the State of ____,
I now pronounce you husband and wife.

You may now kiss!

Final Blessing #5

Now that Bride and Groom
have joined themselves to each other by solemn vows,
and by the giving and receiving of rings,
I do now,
by virtue of the authority vested in me,
pronounce that they are husband and wife.

Final Blessing #6

Now, because you have chosen one another
and pledged to love each other
for all the days of your lives,
before God

and before this loving community of family and friends,
it gives me great joy to pronounce you husband and wife.

Final Blessing #7

Bride and Groom,
I wish you the courage
to keep your loving hearts open to each other
for the rest of your lives,
and to cherish the precious love you share.
May you continue to find delight in each other
and in your being together.
May your love forever nourish you and keep you strong.

I now pronounce that you are husband and wife.

Benediction

Finally, some couples like to end their ceremonies with a Benediction, a final prayer of thanksgiving and sanctification. It can either precede or follow The Kiss. In my experience, when it follows The Kiss, it is often awkward and unexpected for the guests, who are anticipating that the couple will recess after The Kiss. Here are several examples.

Benediction #1

And now in our going,
may the Lord bless you and keep you.
May the Lord be gracious unto you.
Let us rejoice and be glad.
Amen.

Benediction #2

May you endlessly delight one another.
May you love and fulfill each other always.
Go in peace.
Live in joy.
Thanks be to God.

Benediction #3

The Lord bless you and keep you.
The Lord look kindly upon you
and be gracious to you.
The Lord bestow favor upon you
and give you peace.
Amen.

Benediction #4

Bride and Groom,
may the road rise to meet you.
May the wind be always at your back.
May the sun shine warm upon your face,
the rains fall soft upon your fields,
and, until we meet again,
may God hold you in the palm of His hand.

Benediction #5

May your feet be firmly rooted in the earth.
May the air you breathe be sweet and fresh.
May your lives flow together like two streams into a graceful river.
May the flame of spirit burn strong within you.
May you know God's presence in your lives.
And may God bless your life together.

Benediction #6

Beloved God,
source of love, light, and sound,
pour your grace down upon <u>Bride</u> and <u>Groom</u>,
that they may fulfill the vows that they have made today
through their love and faithfulness to each other.

<u>Bride</u> and <u>Groom</u>,
go in peace and love,
seeing in each other the face of God
smiling upon you
and blessing you each and every day.

The Recessional

The Recessional is the end of the ceremony, but it is also the transition to the next activity of the day. Upon recessing, the couple might have a receiving line, or go off to spend a few minutes alone or to have pictures taken while their guests go on to a cocktail hour. As with the Processional, there are details to think through for the Recessional. The sample Recessional Cues and Sequencing Worksheet that follows will serve as an example as you fill out the blank copy found on page 358.

Recessional Cues and Sequencing Worksheet—Sample

Describe the sequencing of the Recessional and where each person will go once they are down the aisle. What will be the cue for the Musicians to begin playing? Will the parents follow the Wedding Party? Will there be a receiving line, and if so, where will it be and who will be in it? Who will be signing the marriage license, when and where will they meet the Officiant?

- *After The Kiss, the Musicians will begin to play and the Bride and Groom will turn and pause so the Photographer can get a picture of them. Then they will walk down the aisle together. They will exit by the door in the right rear of the room to the balcony where they will take their places at the top of the receiving line.*

- *The Maid of Honor and Best Man will come together in front of the Officiant and wait until the Bride and Groom have moved past the last row of guests. The Maid of Honor and Best Man will then recess down the aisle together and wait for the Officiant to sign the marriage license.*

- *After the Maid of Honor and Best Man have passed the last row of guests, the two Flower Girls are next to go down the aisle. As they do so, their mothers will be going down the side aisles to meet them in the back of the room and go together to the balcony area.*

- *The three Bridesmaids and three Groomsmen will recess next, as couples, with the couple nearest the Officiant going first. Each couple will wait in front of the Officiant until the previous couple has passed the last row of guests. They will all go to the balcony area to mingle with the guests.*

- *The parents of the Bride recess next and take their places beside the Bride and Groom in the receiving line.*

- *The parents of the Groom recess next and take their places beside the parents of the Bride in the receiving line.*

- *The Officiant recesses.*

- *The guests follow the Recessional and move to the receiving line.*

6

Incorporating Personal Beliefs and Circumstances

They used to say that the average American family had two and a half children. And, with the exception of some woman who was four and a half months pregnant and had a husband and two children, there was no such thing. With this idea in mind, it is very important to remember that when you are designing your ceremony outside of the context of a specific religious tradition, there is no such thing as the perfect wedding. The bridal magazine imagery of weddings may or may not be appropriate for you. Be bold. Dare to celebrate who you are rather than trying to be something you are not. Rather than looking to marketing images of the perfect wedding day and how that should look, perhaps couples approaching marriage would be better served by hearing the truer stories of real couples and how they created their wedding day. Real people, not models. Real lives, not fairy tales. It seems appropriate to take people and their lives as they are and to celebrate the sheer hope and optimism that is present in the choice that a man and a woman make to be joined in marriage despite all the trials and tribulations of life.

What is important is that, at the end of your day, you feel wonderful about your wedding and are filled with memories of love, family, and friendship that will warm the cockles of your heart for years to come. If that is best accomplished wearing jeans at a back-yard barbecue rather than a Vera Wang gown at the country club, then hopefully you will have the courage to honor and celebrate your own truth. It is so easy to lose sight of yourself in all the planning and accommodating that goes into a wedding. When so many people tell you that you should do it this way or that way, it can be hard to know and honor the truth of your own way.

One of my favorite stories on this theme is about a couple I married one March. They were originally scheduled to be married in November of the previous year, but rescheduled for June. It was to be the perfect wedding the Bride had been programmed to dream of all her life. In February, she called to reschedule their meeting with me to design the ceremony. She had already postponed it once before. Noticing her obvious distress, I asked if she was all right. She blurted out in response that no, she was not all right, and that she was dreading and hating her wedding and just wanted it to be over. The wedding had swallowed her up and she was crying out for help. Indeed, it had become her mother's dream wedding and not her own. I suggested that she might want to pay some attention to her feelings and to consider the fact that this was *her* wedding and she owed it to herself to give herself a wedding day of memories that she would enjoy and treasure.

I told her the story of my neighbors who had a very intimate wedding—just twelve of us in total. The ceremony was in their apple orchard and was very tender. We had dinner in a nearby restaurant and all headed home by about nine in the evening. Despite their plans to take off on a road-trip honeymoon for several days, all they wanted to do was nest in their country home. So that's what they did for three days. Then a month later, they had a big party with all their friends in New York City. It was perfect for them.

Not realizing the impact this story was having on the Bride on the other end of the phone, I was startled by her enthusiastic response that it sounded just perfect to her. She proceeded to cancel the country club wedding and deal with all the fallout with her family, friends, and those she had hired. She and the Groom decided they would have their ceremony the first week in March at one of the mountain houses across the river, but when they checked that out, it wasn't right for them either. By this time, many of us were wondering if, when, and how they would ever get married. The day we designed the ceremony, they had just come from the mountain house and were back at the drawing board, not knowing where or when to hold the ceremony and reception. Off-handedly, I suggested they look at a nearby mansion turned elegant Bed and Breakfast. They loved it and scheduled the ceremony for the end of March. It turned out to be an unseasonably beautiful day and they had a wonderful time with their intimate group of twenty-six family members and friends. Appropriately, they gave their guests T-shirts declaring "I was there" with the couple's names in a heart with doves, and four dates on the bottom with three of them crossed out.

It's sad when our fantasies make us uncomfortable with our truths. One couple asked me to marry them, and it took a while before I was able to get the full story of what their circumstances were. I could feel that they were hiding something. I sensed they were somehow afraid I would judge and reject them for their truth. They had both been married before and technically, he was still married. His first wife had taken their two children to their homeland and was making it very difficult for him to finalize the divorce after several years. Meanwhile he had met and fallen in love with this woman he wanted to marry. They had been living together with her five-year-old daughter from her first marriage for several years when I met them. She had eloped for her first marriage and her father had always been disappointed that he never got to walk her down the aisle. Now her father was dying and time was getting short.

Would I marry them? They understood that legally they could not be married but they didn't want to wait any longer for fear that the father's condition would worsen. We settled on the idea of a commitment ceremony. Essentially, the spirit of the ceremony was identical to that of a marriage, but the term "marriage" was never used and there was no declaration of marriage or signing of a license. But for all intents and purposes, they were married and her father's dream came true. (See Ceremony Nine on page 333.)

Sometimes elements of the ceremony have to be altered to accommodate the couple's circumstances. In one sad story I heard recently, a young Groom had chosen his best friend from childhood to be his Best Man. Two weeks before the ceremony, the guys were all out to lunch together when the Best Man died of a heart condition that no one, including the young man and his family, knew he had. The Groom was, of course, devastated. In seeking to find a balance between the grief of his loss and the joy of his marriage, the Groom chose not to appoint anyone else as Best Man. The deceased young man's parents, who had known the Groom for most of his life, chose to attend the ceremony but not the reception.

Who the Bride and Groom are and what their lives are about covers a wide range today. There are several considerations that I run into frequently when customizing ceremonies to reflect the beliefs and circumstances of the couple. For example, more and more couples today are renewing their vows in five-, ten-, or twenty-five-year increments. And commitment ceremonies, like the one mentioned above, are becoming an alternative to marriage for couples for a variety of reasons. There are also many occasions when a marriage not only joins the couple but also creates a family including children from previous marriages. Some couples also like to include rituals from their religious heritage, even if they are not still practicing that particular faith. Family and religious traditions are also often incorporated into the ceremony. This section will specifically address the special considerations I most frequently encounter. These include features for a smaller wedding, the inclusion of children from a previous marriage in the ceremony, and the incorporation of religious and ethnic traditions.

For a Smaller Wedding

There are certain components of a wedding ceremony that are inappropriate for a large ceremony, but can increase the intimacy of a smaller one. If the Bride and Groom are surrounded by their twenty-five closest family members and friends, they will likely want that familiarity to be reflected in the ceremony. To the degree that it is comfortable for the couple and guests, they may like to actively involve the guests in the celebration. One way this can be done is in the arrangement of the chairs. Forming a circle or curved rows at a more intimate distance than usual can create the desired effect. The fewer guests you have, the more intimate your ceremony can be. For example, some of the things you might consider doing if you have twenty-five or fewer guests include:

- Performing all or part of the ceremony in a circle.
- Passing the wedding rings among the guests to place their blessing on them.
- Having given all participants candles, the light of God can be passed among your guests by having the Officiant light a candle and in turn lighting the candles of the Bride and Groom. They light the candles of the Best Man and Maid of Honor, who pass the light to the next people in the wedding party, who in turn pass it on to each other and then on to the guests.
- Having the guests all bring flowers to the ceremony or have the flowers given to them as they arrive. At the appointed time, they all bring their flowers to the Bride and Groom or place them in a vase when leaving the ceremony site to symbolize the beauty of the couple's love. Another version of this idea would

be to have the couple's nearest and dearest friends and family members all in aisle seats. Having each been given a single rose when they entered, they would hand them to the Bride as she processed, thus creating her wedding bouquet.

The Friendship Circle

One of the ceremonial elements that lends itself to a smaller and more intimate gathering of loved ones is the Friendship Circle. It originates in the Quaker tradition and offers guests the opportunity to share their best wishes for the couple as part of the ceremony itself. For anywhere up to about seventy-five guests, you might want to include this feature.

Depending on the layout, I usually direct the guests to form a circle around the chairs, or nearby, for this portion of the ceremony. Symbolically, the circle is a powerful reminder of the loving support that surrounds the couple. It is a good idea to recruit at least two or three people who will definitely speak up here. Then, once the ice has been broken, it is amazing and very touching how others join in and share from their hearts. You will probably be surprised by who chimes in and the loving thoughts that are expressed. It's a wonderful opportunity for the couple, as part of the circle, to see all their guests and take a few moments to receive the gift of their presence. The circle also breaks the ice among the guests as they have the chance to become better acquainted with one another and are more likely to interact at the reception. However, in order to be successful, this element needs to be a good match with the temperament of the guests. If they are uncomfortable, they might not speak, and the silence can be painful. That's why it is important to make sure that at least a few people plan to speak. On the other hand, discuss with the Officiant ahead of time that you would like him or her to call the sharings to a close if they seem to be going on for too long.

The one thing to be careful about with this element is that it can be very hard to predict how long it will take. In my experience, it usually runs only about five to seven minutes and has rarely exceeded ten to fifteen minutes (but is always well worth the time). However, one couple chose to include the circle in their gathering of over 125 people, and they went on and on and on despite my making several attempts to bring it to a close. The Groom insisted I let it continue, and so it went on for almost an hour. As a result, they had one hour less of the reception they were paying for, not to mention cold food!

I usually set this segment up with a brief introduction such as the following and then just let it follow its own course. When I sense it coming to an end, I ask for any final contributions, thank the guests, and ask everyone to return to their seats.

Friendship Circle #1

<u>Bride</u> and <u>Groom</u> have expressed to me
the importance of actively involving all of you
in their wedding celebration.
We are going to share a ritual,
the Friendship Circle,
that originated in the Quaker tradition.

In a moment, I'm going to ask you all to get up
and form a circle around the chairs.
Then, anyone who wishes to
may share their thoughts and feelings
about <u>Bride</u> and <u>Groom</u> coming together in marriage.
You may want to offer them your blessing
or to share a story about them,
a reflection of a time you have shared together.
Whatever comes forward is just fine.

So now, let us form our circle of family and friends.

When Your Ceremony Involves Children

There are many roles that children can play in your wedding besides the obvious Flower Girl and Ring Bearer. For example, they can distribute things like ceremony programs, wedding favors, bubbles, birdseed, or rice. Depending on their ages and personalities, they can also assist guests in finding the wedding site if it is not in an obvious location. They may also be called upon to greet and escort your guests. Most children love being asked to take candid pictures with a disposable camera.

There are two primary ways that children become part of a marriage ceremony. In the first case, many couples like the idea of having a Flower Girl or Ring Bearer, or multiples of each, and they select them from among their families or those of members of the wedding party. In the second case, it is not uncommon these days for the Bride or the Groom to have children from a previous marriage. This situation can be a very delicate matter and requires careful attention to the child's feelings and circumstances. Some children feel disloyal to their other parent if they participate in or even attend the wedding. Others are eager to be involved because they are becoming part of a new family unit.

Most typically, young children are involved as Flower Girls and Ring Bearers, and older children as junior attendants. Sometimes a child will be asked to read or sing a song. There are also a number of creative ways to acknowledge children who will be part of your new family unit. The Opening Prayer, Gathering Words, and Final Blessing can include statements that acknowledge the creation of a family as well as a marriage, and thus specifically name the children.

To a large extent, the age of the children will dictate your options. For example, with a young child, you might want to have both the Bride and Groom share a vow of love and protection with the child and to give them a gift such as a necklace or ring as a symbol of your promise and your union as a family. Children may also want to say a vow to their new family as well. Here are several examples.

In this first example, the Bride had a five-year-old daughter from a previous marriage.

Involving Children #1

Officiant:
This ceremony marks not only the union
of <u>Groom</u> and <u>Bride</u> as husband and wife,
it also celebrates the combining
of <u>Groom</u> and <u>Bride</u> with her daughter, <u>Child 1</u>,
to form a new family.

(The daughter is invited to join her mother.)

Bride to Daughter:
Because <u>Groom</u> and I are getting married today,
that means we three are becoming more of a family today too.
One reason I decided to marry <u>Groom</u>
is because he cares so deeply for you.
So, today <u>Groom</u> is joining our family
because we love him and we are so happy together.

Groom to Bride's daughter:
<u>Child 1</u>, I am so happy that we are a family.
I want to protect you, to take care of you,
to love you, and to always be your friend.
I give you this necklace as a symbol of my promise
to always be there for you.

(He puts the necklace on her and she sits down.)

In this next version, the Bride and Groom brought five children under age seven together from their previous marriages into their newly formed family.

Involving Children #2
Officiant:

> Today marks not only the marriage of <u>Bride</u> and <u>Groom</u>,
> but the formalizing of the family bond they are creating
> with their children <u>Child 1</u>, <u>Child 2</u>, <u>Child 3</u>, <u>Child 4</u>, and <u>Child 5</u>.

Bride and Groom to Children:
(reading alternating paragraphs)

> <u>Child 1</u>, <u>Child 2</u>, <u>Child 3</u>, <u>Child 4</u>, and <u>Child 5</u>,
> we are now one family, a mom and dad, brothers and sisters.
> Each of you has so much beauty inside.
> You can do anything you choose to do with your life.
>
> We promise to be patient and to support each of you,
> to give you strength and room to grow,
> to do less correcting and more connecting,
> to stop playing serious and to seriously play,
> to do less tugging and do more hugging.
>
> Life is full of surprises,
> and we want you to know
> that no matter what happens,
> no matter what you do or who you become,
> we will always love you.
>
> <u>Child 1</u>, <u>Child 2</u>, <u>Child 3</u>, <u>Child 4</u>, and <u>Child 5</u>,
> today we give you these rings
> to remind you of our love
> and to serve as a symbol of the unity of our new family.

Here is another version in which the Bride and Groom each bring a son to the new family created by their marriage.

Involving Children #3
Officiant:
> This ceremony marks not only the union of <u>Bride</u> and <u>Groom</u>
> as husband and wife,
> but like ripples on the water,
> their union creates new family circles as well.
>
> So we are here also to celebrate
> the combining of <u>Bride</u> and <u>Groom</u>
> with their sons <u>Bride's son</u> and <u>Groom's son</u>
> into a new family created by this marriage.

Bride to Groom's son:
> <u>Groom's son</u>, I feel blessed
> that our families are joining together today
> and that <u>Bride's son</u> and I
> can continue our special friendship with you.
> Even though we will spend time together as a family,
> your time alone with your father is just as important.
> I promise you that will continue.
> I give you this chain as a symbol of my promise
> to be your friend and to always be there for you.

Bride to her son:
> Because <u>Groom</u> and I are getting married today,
> that means we are becoming more of a family today too.
> One reason I decided to marry <u>Groom</u>
> is because he cares so deeply for you.
> So, today <u>Groom</u> is joining our family
> because we love him and we are so happy together.

Groom to Bride's son:

> Bride's son, I am so happy that we are a family.
> I want to protect you, to take care of you,
> to love you, and to always be your friend.
> I give you this ring as a symbol of my promise
> to always be there for you.

Groom to his son:

> Groom's son, you and I will always be special buddies,
> and I want you to know that it means a lot to me
> that you have grown to love Bride and Bride's son too.
> While we will all be a new family together,
> you and I will always have our special friendship.
> I love you forever, buddy.

In this example, the children are called forward to say vows of love and loyalty to their new family after the Bride and Groom exchange their Wedding Vows.

Involving Children #4
Officiant:

> Today, Bride and Groom are joined in their vows
> by Child 1 and Child 2,
> for they too wish to express the love and commitment
> they have given and received,
> and will continue to feel as a part of this family.

> For you, Child 1 and Child 2,
> something very special is happening today.
> In this ceremony, you are sharing in the celebration
> of the happiness that is present in your family,
> and you are affirming your role
> in that most fundamental of all human relationships.

May the joy and excitement of today
and the warmth and loving of your home
also serve as a model for you of what you will seek and find
when it is your time to enter into marriage
and to create your own family.

(The Officiant then asks each child to repeat the following vow):

I, <u>Child 1</u>, do hereby promise to love, honor, and cherish
my family and God,
to always be honest and true about who I am,
and to honor and respect the truth of each member of this family.

(The children return to their seats and then, after the Bride and Groom share rings, the children are again invited up to receive rings as well.)

Officiant:
May I have the children's rings, please?

Bride and Groom:
<u>Child 1</u> and <u>Child 2</u>, we give you these rings today
as tokens of our love for you,
and as a symbol of the unity of our family.

Older children are more likely to be sensitive about participating in the ceremony if their other parent is unhappy about it, especially if still single. These concerns should be honored by all means. It is important to remember that there are many confusing emotions to be processed by children when a parent is getting remarried. Sometimes, more mature children like to write something to read during the wedding ceremony. Again, they should be invited to participate, but never forced to do so.

This next sample is an adaptation of the Candle Ceremony to include children.

Involving Children #5

Officiant:

Bride, Groom, Child 1, and Child 2,
you have all pledged your love to your new family
and promised to love and nurture each other.

Love is something very magical.
It is a gift from God that lights us up inside.
And when a man and a woman
join their hearts together in marriage,
their lights flow together
and a single brighter light goes forth
from their united being.

When a family is formed as an extension of this union,
the light is intensified by the light
that flows from the children as well.
The happiness you feel in being a family together
is a reflection of this.
This light that you have, this happiness,
comes from God.
So when we love one another,
we are experiencing God's presence in our lives.

Bride, Groom, Child 1, and Child 2,
you are divine and eternal beings,
and as you come to know this,
you will never cease to wonder and glory
in your coming together as a family.

By being a loving family,
you will awaken your love for God
and your knowledge of the fact
that within each human being
burns the spark of the divine.

When people love one another
with devotion and freedom,
they kindle the awareness of that spark
in each other
as nothing else quite can do.
<u>Bride</u>, <u>Groom</u>, <u>Child 1</u>, and <u>Child 2</u>,
in joining together today,
you kindle one another's divine light
and promise always to do your best
to see that light in each other
and to nurture and tend that divine flame
in one another
as best you can each day,
especially at the times it may be hardest to do,
and the times when one of you may doubt or forget
the existence of that light within yourself.

INCORPORATING RELIGIOUS TRADITIONS

Many couples like to include rituals or traditions specific to their religious heritage, even if these affiliations are not actively reflected in their current lives. In addressing religious wedding traditions, I have chosen not to attempt to cover all the various religions, but rather have chosen to focus on one religion and show the various ways that it might be woven into a wedding ceremony. Since I receive the most requests for the inclusion of Jewish rituals, I have chosen Judaism to serve as an example. Even if you have no personal affiliation with Judaism, I encourage you to read these passages, as they are quite beautiful and might inspire you to find ways to express your own heritage in your wedding ceremony.

Jewish Wedding Rituals
EXPLANATION OF JEWISH TRADITIONS

This selection can be inserted after the Opening Prayer or Gathering Words to explain the symbolism of the Jewish rituals being included in the ceremony. The chuppah is a ceremonial fabric arch under which the wedding is performed. Some couples rent a chuppah for the occasion, others buy or make one. Some couples ask their guests to contribute to the design of the chuppah by agreeing to decorate a square which will become part of a patchwork of expressions sewn together into the wedding chuppah. This becomes not only the canopy for their wedding ceremony, but a patchwork quilt filled with good wishes and memories of their loved ones to keep in their home. This is reminiscent of the early American friendship quilt made for the Bride by women friends and family members. Particularly when including Jewish rituals, I suggest to couples that they invite a family elder steeped in the tradition to co-officiate this segment of the ceremony with me.

Explanation of Jewish Traditions #1
Officiant:
> Today, along with the wedding of these two people,
> there is a marriage of two religions taking place.
> Two religions, one God.
> Bride and Groom have included some Jewish traditions
> in their ceremony.
> I will explain what the symbols and traditions mean,
> so we can all understand and appreciate the sentiment
> that is being invoked here.

Bride's grandfather, ____, will co-officiate
this part of the ceremony with me.

The first symbol we see today is the chuppah.
It is referred to as the wedding canopy.
The chuppah symbolizes the framework of the home,
whose poles are supported by the friends and family
who stood by the Bride and Groom during their childhood
and are now standing by in loving support
of their marriage union.
The openness of the chuppah
pledges that there shall be no secrets,
and serves to remind the couple
of the importance of openness to one's partner
and to God's centrality in the relationship.
The chuppah's flimsiness reminds the couple
that the only thing that is sturdy about a home
is the people in it who love each other
and choose to be together, to be a family.
The only anchor that they will have
will be holding onto each others' hands.

As guests today,
we are here not only to rejoice
and honor the Bride and Groom,
but also to provide a sustaining community for them.
We give Bride and Groom
the outlines or sketch of a foundation,
but it is up to them
to determine where they want to go
and what they want their life together to be.
For this the Jews say "Mazel tov!"
which means "Good luck!"

The breaking of the glass at the end of the ceremony
is the most recognizable symbol of a Jewish wedding.
It has numerous symbolic undertones.
One is that, in celebration,
there should always be awe and trembling as well.

The breaking of the glass is an expression of hope
for a future free of all violence.
The fragility of the glass
suggests the frailty of human relationships.
Even the strongest love
is subject to disintegration.
In this context,
the glass is broken to "protect" the marriage
with an implied prayer,
"As this glass shatters,
so may the marriage never break."
The shattered glass also serves us all
as a reminder that the world is replete with imperfection
and thus serves as an imperative to us
to partake in the mending of the world.

The breaking of the glass
symbolizes the end of the ceremony,
just after The Kiss.
At that time
I ask you to join me in calling out
"Mazel tov!" or "Congratulations!"

The prevailing sentiment provided
by all the symbols I've talked about
is really a message about human beings

and not religious beings.
Moving out of the sphere of Jewish symbols
and non-Jewish symbols,
as human beings we need community for strength,
past traditions to provide a road map
for how to behave now,
and love to build a future.
Take the symbols of this love,
<u>Bride</u> and <u>Groom</u>,
and indulge in the moment
and your future.
Mazel tov!

(Note: At the end of the ceremony, when the Bride and Groom are kissing, the glass is placed on the ground in front of the Groom who breaks it just after The Kiss.)

BLESSING AND DRINKING THE WINE

The ritual of drinking wine can be placed before the exchange of Wedding Vows with a Co-Officiant saying the prayers in Hebrew, followed by the Officiant echoing them in English, line by line.

Blessing and Drinking the Wine #1

Officiant:

Common to the Jewish wedding ceremony
is to ask God to bless the wedding.
A common prayer used is called Mi Adir:

Co-Officiant:	Officiant:
Mi Adir el hakol	Splendor is upon everything
Mi Baruch el hakol	Blessing is upon everything
Mi Gadol el hakol	Who is full of this abundance
Hey' varesh h'hatan v'kallah	Bless this Groom and Bride

(At this point the Co-Officiant raises the wine glass.)

Officiant:
> The symbol of drinking the wine
> is associated with celebrations, festivals,
> and *simcha* (which means joy).
> Without wine there would be no blessing.
> The act of drinking the wine
> is referred to as kiddush,
> and is part of virtually all Jewish observance
> as a prayer of sanctification.

(At this point the wine is handed to the Groom.)

> *At this time
> I ask <u>Bride</u> and <u>Groom</u> to share this wine
> as <u>Co-Officiant</u> bestows the blessing upon them.

Co-Officiant:	Officiant:
Baruch Ata Adonai	Holy One of the blessing
Eloheyne Melech Ha-olam,	Your presence fills creation,
borey p'ree ha-gaffen.	forming the fruit of the vine.
Amen.	Amen.

(At this point the Co-Officiant sits down.)

Note: It is common practice to have a light bulb prewrapped in a napkin on the table, which is used in place of a glass for the actual "breaking of the glass." This is done because it is easier to break a light bulb and it makes a festive popping sound.

Alternative prayer for the drinking of the wine.

Blessing and Drinking the Wine #1a
Officiant:
> As you share this wine from a single cup,
> so may you, under God's guidance,
> share contentment, peace, and fulfillment
> from the cup of life.
>
> May you find life's joys heightened,
> its bitterness sweetened,
> and each of its moments
> hallowed by true companionship and love.
>
> Blessed are you, Lord, our God,
> King of the universe,
> who creates the fruit of the vine.

THE SEVEN BLESSINGS

Some couples like to include the reading of the seven blessings as part of the Final Blessing after the Ring Exchange. They can be read by one person or assigned to seven guests who rise in their places in turn to read them. This reading is a wonderful way to create participation among more of your guests.

Seven Blessings #1
> 1. Blessed art thou, O Lord our God,
>   Ruler of the universe,
>   Creator of the fruit of the vine.
> 2. Blessed art thou, O Lord our God,
>   Ruler of the universe,
>   Creator of all things to thy glory.

3. Blessed art thou, O Lord our God,
   Ruler of the universe,
   Creator of man and woman.

4. Blessed art thou, O Lord our God,
   Ruler of the universe,
   who creates us to share with You
   in life's everlasting renewal.

5. Blessed art thou, O Lord our God,
   Ruler of the universe,
   who causes Zion to rejoice in her children.

6. Blessed art thou, O Lord our God,
   Ruler of the universe,
   who causes the Bride and Bridegroom to rejoice.

7. Blessed art thou, O Lord our God,
   Ruler of the universe,
   Creator of joy and gladness,
   Bride and Groom,
   love and kinship,
   peace and friendship.
   May there always be heard in the cities of Israel
   and in the streets of Jerusalem:
   the sounds of joy and of happiness,
   the voice of the Groom
   and the voice of the Bride,
   the shouts of young people celebrating,
   and the songs of children at play.
   Blessed art thou, O Lord,
   who causes the Bride and Groom to rejoice together.

PRAYERS FROM THE OLD TESTAMENT

Another Jewish tradition is the inclusion of prayers from the Old Testament. The following selection, for example, can be included as part of the Final Blessing (again involving the Co-Officiant). These readings include one of seven special prayers for the wedding couple, a prayer for special occasions, and a blessing.

Prayers from the Old Testament #1

Grant perfect joy to these loving companions,
as you did to the first man and woman
in the Garden of Eden.
Praised are you, O Lord,
who grants the joy of Bride and Groom.

Blessed is the Lord our God,
Ruler of the universe,
for giving us life,
for sustaining us,
and for enabling us to reach this day of joy.

This is the day the Lord has made;
let us rejoice and be glad in it.

The Lord bless you and keep you;
the Lord look kindly upon you
and be gracious to you;
the Lord bestow favor upon you
and give you peace.
Amen.

Symbolic Gestures

Finally, two symbolic gestures used in the Jewish tradition are the Ketubah, or Wedding Contract, and having both the Bride and Groom escorted by their parents as part of the Processional. The Ketubah is a written copy of the Wedding Vows and is usually enlarged and decoratively displayed near the ceremony site. It is signed by the couple and sometimes the guests are invited to sign it as well. The second custom is for the parents of the Groom and Bride to escort them both up the aisle. This ritual is now being used by many non-Jewish couples as well.

Incorporating Ethnic Traditions

In addition to including rituals of religious heritage, many couples like to reflect their ethnic traditions. One way this is done is by wearing ethnic clothing. For example, the Scotsman would wear a dress kilt, a Chinese Bride might wear a kimono or simply have red bows on her dress. There are also some wonderful rituals that can be included. For example, in Bermuda, the wedding cake is topped with a tree sapling that the newlyweds can plant at their home and watch grow alongside their marriage. In Korea, ducks (who mate for life), are included in the Processional. In India, the Groom's brother sprinkles the couple with flower petals during the Recessional to ward off evil spirits. Three specific ethnic rituals and their text are included below.

Greek Crowning Ceremony and Common Cup

Two ceremonial rituals that come out of the Greek Orthodox tradition are the crowning of the Bride and Groom and the drinking from a common cup. In the version presented here, the text has been altered in an effort to give it greater contemporary appeal without sacrificing the essential meaning of the rituals. The couple's religious sponsor, called Koumbaro (male) or Koumbara (female), serves as an important witness to the union.

Crowning Ceremony #1

Officiant:

In the Greek Orthodox tradition,
the blessing and exchange of crowns
is an essential element of the wedding ceremony.
Just as monarchs are crowned
and charged with the welfare of their realm,
so are the Bride and Groom crowned
and vested with the authority and responsibility
to care for one another's well-being.
Symbolically, each marriage is a kingdom unto itself,
which can lead the couple to God's Heavenly Kingdom
by living with forbearance, compassion,
righteousness, respect, and loving.
The crowns are traditionally kept in the home
to remind the couple of their responsibility and commitment
to live by good Christian values
in their marriage kingdom.

Let us pray.

Beloved God,
we ask that you extend to <u>Groom</u> and <u>Bride</u>
the same blessing
you extended to Abraham and Sarah,
Isaac and Rebekah,
Jacob and Rachel,
Moses and Zipporah,
Joakim and Anna,
and Zacharias and Elizabeth.

We ask your blessing
for <u>Groom</u> and <u>Bride</u>'s parents,

who nourished them
and for all of their family and friends
who surround them with their love.

Beloved God,
we ask that you bless <u>Groom</u> and <u>Bride</u>,
that they may perpetuate
the lineage of your love.
We ask that through the grace of the Holy Spirit,
who <u>Groom</u> and <u>Bride</u> are,
where they come from,
their likes, dislikes,
skills, talents, and characteristics
will all be brought into a harmonized oneness
whereby the two become one flesh.
May these crowns serve to remind them
to bring your kingdom here to earth
in their marriage.

(The Officiant places a crown on the Groom's head.)
    As a servant of God,
    I crown you <u>Groom</u> to <u>Bride</u>
    in the Name of the Father
    and of the Son
    and of the Holy Spirit.

(The Officiant places a crown on Bride's head.)
    As a servant of God,
    I crown you <u>Bride</u> to <u>Groom</u>
    in the Name of the Father
    and of the Son
    and of the Holy Spirit.

(The couple's sponsor exchanges the crowns three times, moving them back and forth over the Groom's and Bride's heads while the Officiant repeats the following statement three times.)

> O Lord our God,
> crown <u>Groom</u> and <u>Bride</u>
> with honor and with glory.

This ritual is usually followed by a recitation of the Lord's Prayer (see page 253) and then the sharing of the Common Cup.

(As the Officiant speaks, the Groom and Bride each take three sips of wine.)

Common Cup #1
Officiant:
> <u>Groom</u> and <u>Bride</u>,
> as you drink from this common cup of wine,
> you drink from the cup of life
> as husband and wife.
> From this day forward
> you will share life's bitterness
> with its sweetness,
> its disappointment
> with its happiness,
> and its tribulation
> with its joy.
> From this moment forward
> you will share everything,
> doubling your joys
> and dividing your sorrows.

The Polish Ritual of Symbolic Gifts

A Polish wedding tradition involves the parents of the Bride and Groom giving the couple symbolic gifts. It is traditionally done during the wedding reception, but can also be incorporated in the ceremony as described in the following text.

Symbolic Gifts #1

Officiant:

> Bride and Groom's parents are going to join us now
> for a cherished Polish tradition,
> which has been passed down through the centuries.
> It involves the symbolic sharing
> of bread, salt, wine, and a silver coin.

> As their parents give Bride and Groom each a piece of bread,
> we wish: "May you never go hungry or be in need."

> As they are given a sip of wine,
> we wish: "Enjoy the sweetness of life with good health,
> good cheer, and the company of good friends."

> As they each place a speck of salt on their tongue
> we wish: "May you overcome the bitterness of life."

> As they are given a silver coin
> to hold between their right hands together,
> we wish: "May you be wealthy and abundant."

> Finally, Bride and Groom's parents kiss them
> as a welcome to the family
> and as a sign of their love and unity.

(Parents return to their seats.)

The Wrapping of the Mantilla

In Spain, the bridal couple is wrapped in a large scarf, or mantilla, by their parents.

Mantilla #1

Officiant:

> The wrapping of the mantilla
> around the Bride and Groom by their parents
> is the traditional Spanish symbol
> of two families uniting as one
> in the love shared by their children.

> Today, we are witnessing a beautiful expression
> of commitment, unity, and dreams coming true
> as <u>Bride</u> and <u>Groom</u> become wife and husband.

> At this time, I ask <u>Bride's parents</u> and <u>Groom's parents</u>
> to place the mantilla around their children
> in what is hoped will be the first of many traditions
> that will hold this newly formed family
> as one loving unit for generations to come.

(The parents wrap the mantilla around the couple for a few moments and then the mothers fold it and the Bride's mother takes it with her to her seat.)

Part Three

Putting It All Together

The following selection of ceremonies was created primarily from the material presented in Part Two. Each one is an intimate portrait of a couple and their life circumstances. While some have references to Christianity or Judaism, no ceremonies can be labeled as coming from any particular religious tradition. Rather, they are a collection of spiritual wedding celebrations that have been written from the hearts of the couples. Each ceremony is a patchwork of prose and rituals that resonate with the couple's beliefs, values, style, and circumstances. You might want to avoid the temptation to skip reading a particular ceremony based on its label or a first impression that it is not for you. Each one has a wonderful variety of elements well worth exploring. Besides, it's always a good idea to take a glimpse at how others go about marrying—both as a means of expansion and a confirmation that you are choosing the right way for you.

Each ceremony is followed by a text worksheet that identifies the passages used from Part Two of this book. The worksheet will assist you in cross-referencing the various ceremonial elements used in each sample ceremony.

7

Sample Ceremonies

Ceremony One:
Spiritual and Heartfelt

OPENING PRAYER

Let us begin
by welcoming the presence of God
within each of us.
As we lift into the loving
that joins us together as one,
let us surround <u>Bride</u> and <u>Groom</u>
with our love, our prayers,
and our best wishes for them
on this, their wedding day,
and throughout their journey together
as husband and wife.

Beloved God,
we welcome you
and are so grateful for your presence

here with us today.
We have come here as a community
of family and friends
to love and support <u>Bride</u> and <u>Groom</u>,
to witness their entrance
into the sacred and joyous covenant of marriage,
and to celebrate the beginning of their journey together
as husband and wife.

We are here because we love <u>Bride</u> and <u>Groom</u>.
We rejoice that they have found each other
and that through each other,
they have come to know the power of love
as they have never known it before.

We celebrate this union
of their hearts, minds, bodies, and souls
and wish them great joy.

We ask, Beloved God,
that you guide and bless <u>Bride</u> and <u>Groom</u>
with a loving, healthy, and happy marriage.
We ask that through this union
they may come to know you more deeply.
Amen.

REMEMBRANCE

<u>Bride</u> and <u>Groom</u>
have asked that we take a moment
to honor the memory of those loved ones
who could only be here today in spirit.

GATHERING WORDS

Dearly beloved,
we are gathered here
in the presence of these witnesses,
to join together this man and this woman
in holy matrimony;
which is an honorable estate,
revered since time immemorial
as the most profound and tender
of human relationships.

The union of husband and wife
in heart, body, and mind
is intended by God
for their mutual joy;
for the help and comfort given one another
in prosperity and adversity,
and, when it is God's will,
for the procreation of children
and their nurture
in the knowledge and love of the Lord.

Therefore marriage is not to be entered into
unadvisedly or lightly,
but reverently, deliberately,
and in accordance with the purposes
for which it was instituted by God.

<u>Bride</u> and <u>Groom</u>,
remember that love and faithfulness alone
will provide a solid foundation
for a long and happy marriage.

No relationship is more tender
than that of husband and wife.
And no promises are more sacred
than those of marriage partners.
In keeping faithfully to your vows
and in bringing to this marriage
the best that is within you,
your life together will be filled with grace and joy,
and your home will be a place of peace.

The choice to enter into marriage is profound.
In choosing a lifelong partner,
we are choosing the one
who will witness our changes and growth,
and who will affect these changes
and shape our maturation as well.

<u>Bride</u> and <u>Groom</u>,
this day not only signifies a celebration
of shared values and commitment,
but it attests to the fact
that you have chosen to build your future together.
Through the sacred vows of marriage
you are saying that who you are
and who you want to be
can best be achieved through this union.

As we rejoice in <u>Bride</u> and <u>Groom</u>'s marriage today,
let us each consecrate the relationships in our own lives
and rededicate ourselves to these unions we share.
Let us each choose the path of loving and caring
for one another

and of making these commitments
a priority in our lives.

DECLARATION OF SUPPORT

<u>Bride</u> and <u>Groom</u>,
today we have come together
to celebrate the love you have found with each other.
By being here with you,
each of us is declaring our support
for your decision to join together in marriage.

(To guests)

As families and friends
you form the community of support
that surrounds <u>Bride</u> and <u>Groom</u>.
Each of you, by your presence here today,
is being called upon to uphold them
in honoring and loving each other.

Always stand beside them,
never between them.
Offer them your love and support,
not your judgment.
Encourage them with your kindness and loving hearts,
and honor this marriage
into which they have come to be joined today.

Will everyone please stand?

Collectively, you represent
the families, friends, and traditions
that have brought <u>Bride</u> and <u>Groom</u>
to this point in their lives.

Please affirm your support for this marriage
by responding "Yes, I do"
to the following question:

As part of the community
which surrounds <u>Bride</u> and <u>Groom</u>,
do you offer your love and support
to strengthen their marriage
and bless this family
created by their union?

Guests: Yes, I do!

Please be seated.

MARRIAGE ADDRESS

Marriage is the essence of human relationships.
It challenges us to be of one accord
without abandoning the truth of our individuality.
It challenges us to not lose ourselves in one another,
but rather to walk side by side
heading in the same direction.
As with all relationships,
marriage is an endless presentation of choices
about how we want to be with one another.
Each choice results
in either more unity or more separation.
Choose into that unity,
<u>Bride</u> and <u>Groom</u>,
every chance you get.

Sacrifice your judgments, expectations,
and any other ways

that you have learned
to separate yourselves from each other.

Share the gifts of your friendship, humor,
vulnerability, sensitivity, and kindness.
Be sure to find ways each day
to protect, affirm, and support each other,
and to treasure the balance and shared values
that you have found with each other.

Enjoy the intertwining
of your independence with your intimacy.
I wish you the courage
to keep your loving hearts open to each other
for the rest of your lives.
God bless you.

CANDLE CEREMONY

From every human being there rises a light
that reaches straight to heaven.
And, when two souls who are destined to be together
find each other,
their streams of light flow together,
and a single brighter light
goes forth from their united being.
Human love is not a substitute for spiritual love—
it is an extension of it.

Bride and Groom,
when you see each other
as the divine and eternal beings that you are,
you will never cease to wonder and glory

in your coming together.
The purpose of human love
is to awaken love for God.
The truth that is continually reborn
is that within each human being
burns the spark of the divine.
When two people love one another
with devotion and freedom,
they kindle the awareness of that spark in each other
as nothing else quite can do.

Bride and Groom,
in committing to one another today,
you kindle one another's divine light
and promise always to do your best
to see that light in one another,
to nurture and tend that divine flame
in your partner
as best you can each day,
especially at the times it may be hardest to do,
and the times your partner may doubt or forget
the existence of that light
within him or herself.

Bride, take this candle now,
and light it from the center candle
representing the divine source.
As you do so,
symbolically enter the sacred trust
to honor the divine spirit in Groom.

Groom, as you light this candle
from the divine source,

symbolically enter the sacred trust
to honor the divine spirit in <u>Bride</u>.

Now, bring your individual flames together,
symbolizing the new and greater flame of your marriage,
remembering that just as this union is made stronger
by your strength as individuals,
so are you as individuals
made stronger by the strength of this union.

And never forget
that the light of your union,
while made up of your unique
and individual expressions of light,
is continually sustained and renewed
by your connection to the eternal
and inexhaustible light of God, the Source.

(To guests)
Please stand and join me in the Lord's Prayer.

THE LORD'S PRAYER

Our Father, who art in heaven,
hallowed be thy name.
Thy kingdom come,
Thy will be done,
On earth as it is in heaven.
Give us this day our daily bread,
and forgive us our trespasses,
As we forgive those
who trespass against us.
And lead us not into temptation,

but deliver us from evil,
For thine is the kingdom,
the power,
and the glory forever.
Amen.

WEDDING VOWS

Bride and Groom,
please join hands to share your Wedding Vows.

Groom:
I take you, Bride, to be my wife,
from this day forward,
to join with you
and share all that is to come.
To laugh with you in joy,
to grieve with you in sorrow,
to grow with you in love,
serving mankind in peace and hope,
as long as we both shall live.

Bride:
I choose you, Groom, to be my lifelong partner,
lover, and best friend.
I will always be faithful to you
and be at your side
to laugh with you in times of joy
and comfort you in times of sorrow.
Wherever our path leads us,
it takes us together.

I will encourage and support you,
honor and love you.

I will respect our differences
and do my part
to work through all our challenges.

Groom, I'll be your safe haven
and your home.
With purity of heart
and love in my soul,
I stand before our loved ones
as your lifelong partner.

RING EXCHANGE

May I have the rings, please?

Bride and Groom,
these wedding rings
symbolize the holiness, perfection, and peace
that is available to you in your marriage.
They are symbols of the love, friendship,
and faithfulness that you share.

As circles,
they have no beginning or end.
They are round like the sun,
the moon, the earth, and the universe.

Just as these rings
have no points of weakness,
may your union be strong,
and may you be blessed with joy
as you journey through life together
surrounded by the circle of your love.

<u>Groom</u>, place this ring on <u>Bride</u>'s finger.

Groom:
    I love you.
    (He places the ring up to the knuckle of her finger.)

Bride:
    I wed you.
    (She moves the ring over the knuckle onto her finger.)

Officiant:
    <u>Bride</u>, place this ring on <u>Groom</u>'s finger.

Bride:
    I love you.
    (She places the ring up to the knuckle of his finger.)

Groom:
    I wed you.
    (He moves the ring over the knuckle onto his finger.)

FINAL BLESSING
    <u>Bride</u> and <u>Groom</u>,
    you have declared your intention and vows
    before God
    and this gathering of your families and friends.
    May the grace of this day
    carry forward with you
    all the days of your lives.
    May you find delight in each other
    and may your love continue to grow
    and to nurture you
    throughout your lives.

I wish you the strength
to be true to the vows
you have made here today.
May you always have the wisdom
to cherish the precious love you share.
May you abide by the laws of Spirit,
nurturing yourselves and this marriage
with acceptance, understanding,
cooperation, and loving.

May the life you share
be peaceful, healthy, and filled
with blessings and joy.

As the Apache Wedding Blessing declares:

Now you will feel no rain,
for each of you will be shelter to the other;
Now you will feel no cold,
for each of you will be warmth to the other;
Now there will be no loneliness,
for each of you will be companion to the other.
Now you are two persons,
but there is one life before you.
Go now to your dwelling place
to enter into the days of your togetherness,
And may your days be good and long upon the earth.

And now,
by the power vested in me by the State of _____,
I witness and affirm your union of love
and now pronounce you husband and wife.

You may now kiss as husband and wife
for the first time.
Congratulations and God bless you!

Ceremony One: Spiritual and Heartfelt—Text Worksheet

Opening Prayer:
#1, page 75; #3, page 76

Remembrance:
#2, page 107

Gathering Words:
#2, lines 1–6, page 83; #9, paragraph 1, pages 88–89; #12,
paragraph 5, page 93; #10, paragraph 2, page 90; #12,
paragraph 4, page 92; #18, page 97

Declaration of Support:
#1, page 117; #6, page 124

Marriage Address:
#1, pages 126–127

Candle Ceremony:
#1, pages 138–140

Prayer:
The Lord's Prayer

Wedding Vows:
    Groom: #3, lines 1–4, page 156; #4, lines 2–6, page 157
    Bride: #20, page 164

Ring Exchange:
    Prelude: #8, page 197
    Ring Exchange: #1, page 199

Final Blessing:
#1, with Apache Wedding Blessing, pages 203–204

Ceremony Two:
Short and Sophisticated

GATHERING WORDS

Welcome.
A wedding is such a wonderful occasion,
filled with hopes, dreams, and excitement.
We are here today to celebrate the love
that <u>Bride</u> and <u>Groom</u> have for each other,
and to recognize and witness their decision
to journey forward in their lives
as marriage partners.

We are gathered to support them
as they embark upon their voyage of discovery
as husband and wife.
We are here to see them off on this journey.
Let us also be there for them to see them through.

DECLARATION OF SUPPORT

Collectively,
you represent the families, friends, and traditions
that have brought <u>Bride</u> and <u>Groom</u>
to this point in their lives.
Please affirm your support for this marriage
by responding "Yes, I do"
to the following question:

As part of the community
that surrounds <u>Bride</u> and <u>Groom</u>,

do you offer your love and support
to strengthen their marriage
and bless this family
created by their union?

Guests: Yes, I do.

Wedding Vows

Bride and Groom,
please join hands
and share your Wedding Vows.

Groom:

Bride, I promise to love you,
to cherish you,
and to respect you in all ways, always.

I promise to participate fully
in our marriage partnership.
I will give completely
of my mind, body, heart, and soul.

I promise to make your plans and dreams
as important to me as my own.
I promise to do my share
so that our lives together
can be healthy, happy,
and abundantly satisfying.

I promise to lovingly fulfill these vows
each and every day
for all of my days.

Bride:

> <u>Groom</u>, I promise to love you,
> to cherish you,
> and to respect you
> in all ways, always.
>
> I promise to participate fully
> in our marriage partnership.
> I will give completely
> of my mind, body, heart, and soul.
>
> I promise to make your plans and dreams
> as important to me as my own.
> I promise to do my share
> so that our lives together
> can be healthy, happy,
> and abundantly satisfying.
>
> I promise to lovingly fulfill these vows
> each and every day
> for all of my days.

Ring Exchange

Officiant:

> May I have the rings, please?
> <u>Groom</u>, place this ring on <u>Bride</u>'s finger.

Groom:

> <u>Bride</u>, this ring is a symbol
> of the strength and beauty of our love.
> May it belong to your hand
> as my heart belongs to you,

separate yet close,
simple yet miraculous.

Officiant:
Bride, place this ring on Groom's finger.

Bride:
Groom, this ring is a symbol
of the strength and beauty of our love.
May it belong to your hand
as my heart belongs to you,
separate yet close,
simple yet miraculous.

Final Blessing
Now, because you have chosen one another
and pledged to love each other
for all the days of your lives,
before God
and before this loving community
of family and friends,
it gives me great joy
to pronounce you husband and wife.

You may now kiss!

Gathering Words:
#1, page 83; #7, paragraph 2, lines 2–5, page 88

Declaration of Support:
#6, page 124

Wedding Vows:
#12, pages 160–161

Ring Exchange:
#13, page 202

Final Blessing:
#6, pages 207–208

Ceremony Three: Incorporating Your Story

OPENING PRAYER

Let us come into the quiet of prayer.
Beloved and Eternal God,
we are here to celebrate
the marriage of <u>Bride</u> and <u>Groom</u>.

We pray that they each may find
a depth of kindness, caring,
and joy through this union
that will serve as a safe haven for them
as they journey through their lives together.

We also pray that together they may build a life
that brings them balance,
health, and great learning
as they venture
through the trials and triumphs to come.
May they strengthen their bond of love
and find a gentle peacefulness
in being together hand in hand.

And finally, Beloved,
for those of us who are here with our partners today,
we ask for a blessing of renewal and devotion
to the vows we have made.
May we comfort each other with our love
today and every day.
God bless us all.

GATHERING WORDS

As an ecumenical minister,
one of my basic beliefs
is in the importance of unconditional loving.
That means that we love others
not because they are handsome or rich
or only do what we like,
but we love them no matter what they say or do.
Our loving is not conditioned
by the other person's behavior,
but rather it pours forward
from a wellspring of loving
that we tap into inside of ourselves.
We choose to love them
through good times and bad—
just the way the classic wedding vows suggest.

Those of us who are fortunate enough
to heal our misconceptions about loving,
learn that real, true, and sustainable love
comes forth from within,
rather than in reaction to others.
Ever so rarely,
we meet a person who radiates love,
and we just want to be around them.

Those of us who are most fortunate
are able to express unconditional loving
and to find a wonderful partner
who can do that also—
that's where the true magic of love comes in.
Today, we all have the privilege

of witnessing and celebrating
the union of two such people.

Bride and Groom have a love story
that is filled with wisdom
and inspiration for us all.
So let me tell you their story.

Once upon a time
there was a little white girl named Bride,
and a little black boy named Groom,
who went to the same school,
where her father was principal.
When they were in fifth grade,
Groom first saw Bride at a softball game,
and he started watching for her everywhere he went.

In sixth grade,
they were in the same class
and Groom knew that this was the girl for him
and that someday,
they would be boyfriend and girlfriend.
He told his friends this
and they, of course, told him he was crazy.
But Groom wasn't crazy,
and he was very patient.
Bride still didn't realize it,
but Groom was always keeping his eye on her.

They became good friends until the ninth grade
when Bride wrote Groom a letter
to let him know

that she wanted to be his girlfriend.
Then, on October 28, 1983,
he asked her out
and she said yes!

There were no games—
they knew that they were boyfriend and girlfriend.
And it didn't take long before they realized
that they wanted to spend
the rest of their lives together.

They simply loved each other,
and shared a powerful commitment to that love
that carried them through
good times and bad times
in a world filled with challenges,
including racial prejudice
and rules about who should be with whom.
But the fact that the chemical composition of their skin tones
was different
mattered to them about as much
as having different blood types and eye colors.

Over the years,
not only did they see
beyond society's barriers and challenges,
they also served as an example to others
who learned through them
how to do that as well.

So, why didn't they just get married many years ago?
I wondered.
And so I asked.

Bride never thought that Groom would propose
and, while that might not have made sense to others,
it was OK with Bride.
She knew they would always be together
and that was what she wanted most of all.

Meanwhile, Groom knew he had some feelings
he needed to heal within himself
before he could be as secure and confident
as he wanted to be
as a black man entering marriage
with a white woman
in this world of ours.
And so, he set about working things through.
And Bride was patient.

Then, on October 22, 2000,
he went out, bought a ring,
and asked her parents' permission.
He got down on his knee
and proposed to Bride,
and she cried and cried and cried . . .
and of course she said yes.

And so here we are, one year later,
and Bride and Groom are getting married
after an eighteen-year journey
of following their hearts together.
They still get all excited
and filled with butterflies
when they see each other
at the end of the workday,

and they still are best friends.
They have learned to rely on each other
to make themselves stronger and better people.

How blessed we all are
to be here with <u>Bride</u> and <u>Groom</u> today
to celebrate the power of their love
and their union as husband and wife.

This world of ours needs all the love it can get.
So let us learn through <u>Bride</u> and <u>Groom</u>'s example
and let us all do everything we can
to support them in keeping the flame of their love
vibrant and radiant.

REMEMBRANCES AND ACKNOWLEDGMENTS

There are many special people
who are unable to be here with us today
for one reason or another.
So let us call them forward in our hearts.

We would especially like to remember
<u>Groom</u>'s paternal grandparents,
_____ and _____,
who were unable to make the trip,
and <u>Bride</u>'s maternal grandfather, _____,
who has passed away.

We also remember at this time
three people through whom
<u>Bride</u> and <u>Groom</u> witnessed and experienced
inspirational commitment and love:
_____, _____, and _____.

We welcome their presence here with us today
and celebrate their places in our lives.

Marriage Address

Marriage is a magnificent opportunity
to share one's life with another
and to enjoy the adventures
inherent in this most intimate of human relationships.
Today, we gather here
to rejoice with and for Bride and Groom
as they embark on this voyage of discovery.

Bride and Groom,
from this day forward,
this date, October 22nd,
will always have special meaning for you
as the day you vowed to love and to cherish each other
in all ways, always.

Each year when you come upon your anniversary,
I encourage you to rededicate yourselves
to the vows you make here today.
Take stock of where you are in your marriage
and how you are doing as marriage partners.
Express your gratitude to each other
for the ways that you have effectively loved
and supported one another,
and forgive yourselves and each other
for any judgments that have come between you.

Show each other that you can be trusted and counted on
and that you will be a comfort

The Wedding Ceremony Planner

when facing difficult times.
Celebrate abundantly the successes and joys
life brings your way.
Let your love lead the way
and be more important
than anything else.
Then your lives together
will be filled with blessings and joy.

CANDLE CEREMONY

Within each human being
burns the spark of the divine light
that illuminates us all.

As <u>Bride</u> and <u>Groom</u>'s mothers
light their candles,
we are reminded of the faith, wisdom, and love
that have been passed on to <u>Bride</u> and <u>Groom</u>
from the generations before them.
Each generation has passed on their light
through the mystery of two becoming one.
And here again today,
we witness the gathering light
as two families become one.

As they light <u>Bride</u> and <u>Groom</u>'s candles,
they pass their heritage
into this newly forming family
and once again
two become one.
And finally,
as <u>Bride</u> and <u>Groom</u> light the Unity Candle,

they are symbolically stepping
onto the shared path of their marriage.
May their love for each other
grow deeper each day.
And may they tend this union well
so they may enjoy the fruits of its harvest—
abiding in peace, joy, and happiness.

READING BY BRIDE'S FATHER

All good things come to those who wait...
and wait...and wait...and wait...and wait.

Which is exactly what <u>Bride</u> and <u>Groom</u> have done
for eighteen years.
They have both overcome many obstacles and barriers
in their years together.
Their bond of togetherness and love
helped them to get through it all.
They sailed on uncharted waters,
stormy at times,
but when the clouds lifted—
their love was still intact.

I learned from <u>Bride</u> what it is to give,
to love, to care, to understand,
and to commit to what you really want
while letting nothing stand in your way.
She believed in herself and in <u>Groom</u>,
and created a beautiful relationship
that will stand the test of time.

They will confront all their trials and tribulations
and meet those challenges head-on together.
They will continue to break down barriers—
not physical, but mental.
They will help us to understand
what it means to care for someone
and love them so dearly
that no sacrifice would be too great.
They have opened our hearts and minds
to their love and commitment to each other.

<u>Bride</u> is not only a beautiful, intelligent person,
but she is also a unique individual—
always ready to help,
always ready to keep the peace.

I am proud to know <u>Groom,</u>
an individual who has also broken down barriers
and overcome difficulties
to make his dreams come true;
never giving up until he found what he wanted,
always trying to improve himself and do better,
never being satisfied with what is,
but rather what should be.

I love them both dearly,
and will do all I can
to help them continue in their lives,
and thank them for allowing <u>Bride's mother</u> and me
to be part of their lives.

God bless you both.

Wedding Vows

Officiant:

> Bride and Groom,
> please join hands now
> and share your vows.

Groom:

> I have known you
> since the beginning of time, Bride,
> and loved you longer still.
> I am so happy and blessed
> that I found you here in this life.
>
> I promise you
> that I will never take this great love for granted;
> I will always nurture our love
> and be awed by its power.
>
> I vow to you that every day,
> I will hold this marriage sacred,
> for you are the greatest gift of my life.

Bride:

> Groom, when I look at you,
> I see my dreams have come true.
> I feel so blessed every day
> you are in my life.
> After all these years,
> I still get excited
> to hear your voice on the phone
> or to see you after being apart.

You are my best friend,
and we've been through it all together.
You help me feel safe when I am scared.
You help me laugh when I am sad.
You comfort me when I am hurting.
You reassure me when I am doubting.

These past eighteen years with you
have been so wonderful.
The bond we have built between us is so strong,
I know that nothing can weaken it.
For all that you have done for me
and given to me over the years,
I promise to do the same for you.

All I ask of you
is to have faith in us
and to let the love we share
continue to surround you.
Groom, as I stand here before you,
know this:
you have my heart
and I will be yours
and stand by you through eternity.
You are my love.

RING EXCHANGE

Officiant:

May I have the rings, please?

Rings are adornments,
carefully chosen for their beauty and simplicity.
They quietly sit upon our fingers,

reminding us of the power of love
and the pledge of the wearer to his or her partner
to be faithful and true,
and to nurture their love
so it will last a lifetime.

Bride and Groom,
may these rings be for you always
your most treasured adornment,
and may the love they symbolize
be your most treasured possession.

Groom, place this ring on Bride's finger.

Groom:
This ring is my gift to you.
May it always remind you
that from this day forward
you will be surrounded by my love.

Officiant:
Bride, place this ring on Groom's finger.

Bride:
This ring is my gift to you.
May it always remind you
that from this day forward
you will be surrounded by my love.

FINAL BLESSING
Bride and Groom,
our best wishes go forward from this day with you.

We wish for you a fulfilling life,
rich in caring and in happiness.
We wish for you a gentle and peaceful life
that nurtures and comforts you.
We wish for you a noble life,
which reflects your honesty,
kindness, and integrity.
We wish for you an adventuresome life,
exploring the fullness of your own
and each other's true selves.

<u>Bride</u> and <u>Groom</u>,
there is a wonderful life ahead of you.
Live it fully.
Love its changes and choices.
Let life amaze you
and bring you great joy.

And now, by the power vested in me
by the _____ church
and by the State of ____,
I pronounce you husband and wife.

You may now kiss!

Opening Prayer:
#4, page 77

Gathering Words:
#22, page 101

Remembrances and Acknowledgments:
#3, page 107

Marriage Address:
#5, pages 132–133

Candle Ceremony:
#6, pages 147–148

Reading:
A Reading by the Bride's Father

Wedding Vows:
  Groom: #22, page 166
  Bride: #21, pages 165–166

Ring Exchange:
  Prelude #6, pages 196–197
  Ring Exchange #9, page 201

Final Blessing:
#4, pages 206–207

Ceremony Four:
Inspired by Nature

GATHERING WORDS

We are gathered here in this beautiful place
to witness the joining of <u>Bride</u> and <u>Groom</u> in marriage.
They particularly wanted to invite you here
because their sense of spirituality
and the growth of their love
is connected to this place.
They wanted to share with you
the beauty of these mountains
because this is where they have made their home.

During their seven and a half years together,
they've come here on many mornings like this one,
and walked quietly through the mountain laurel,
listening to the wind in the pines.
Their time spent in nature,
climbing some of the mountains
you see before you here,
has been a time of connectedness,
of shared reverence for the world,
and a deepening respect
and love for one another.

It is this sense of timelessness and peace
that they wanted to share with you
on this, their wedding day.

As you look out over the mountains,
please take a moment for reflection
and quiet prayer
to open your hearts and minds
to the love and togetherness
we are here to share
through this ceremony.
You may also want to take a moment
to remember those loved ones
who are not with us today.

DECLARATION OF SUPPORT

Today, we form a circle of love
around <u>Bride</u> and <u>Groom</u>
as they enter into marriage.
To last, their marriage must be a consecration
of each to the other,
and of both to the wider community
of which they are a part.
That community starts with each and every one of you,
their loved ones.
Through their act of marriage,
<u>Bride</u> and <u>Groom</u> have gathered you around them
like a comforting blanket,
forming their community of love and support
as they move forward into a shared life
as marriage partners.

Now, let us share in a moment
of silently extending our blessings
to <u>Bride</u> and <u>Groom</u>
for a loving, healthy, and happy marriage.

<u>Bride</u> and <u>Groom</u>, it is very special
that you have chosen to celebrate your marriage union
in the circle of your families.
I would like to welcome each member of your families.

*(Family members are each called by name, given a flower by the Bride and Groom, and
then, one by one, join into a circle around the Bride and Groom.)*

This circle of your family
represents your circle of loving, caring,
friendship, and family support.
These people embody the traditions and values
that have brought you to this point in your lives.

<u>Bride</u> and <u>Groom</u>, at this time,
your parents would like to share
their best wishes with you.

Bride's mother:
<u>Bride</u>, your father and I are so happy for you today
and filled with pride and joy
that our baby girl
has become such an accomplished and lovely woman.
And, as though that were not enough,
you have found a profound love with <u>Groom</u>
and brought this magnificent young man into our family.

Bride's father:
<u>Groom</u>, I never imagined there would come a day
when I could sincerely feel that anyone
was wonderful enough for our <u>Bride</u>.
But you have changed all that.

She has chosen wisely,
and we are delighted to have you in our family.

Bride's mother:
Bride and Groom,
we have had the good fortune
to build and enjoy
a secure and nurturing marriage.
Our greatest wish for you
is that you too have the good fortune
to share a healthy and happy marriage,
and that you continue
to light up the room for each other
for the rest of your lives.

Groom's mother:
My dear son Groom,
nothing could give your father and me greater pleasure
than to stand here with you today
knowing that you have found
what your generation calls your soul mate.
I have watched you and Bride
really take your time in getting to know each other
and in building a solid foundation
of love and respect for each other.
And now, as you stand on the threshold of your marriage,
I can truly say
we support you both without reservation
and with great enthusiasm.

Groom's father:

I remember when <u>Groom</u> was a young boy
and used to love learning
all the names of the trees, flowers, and birds.
Now I listen to the two of you
share your anecdotes and lessons from nature
and am so pleased for you both
that you share this common bond.
Seeing how much you two love and understand nature
touches me deeply.
You are a wise and wonderful pair,
and you make us all better people
just by knowing you.
May God bless you always.

Officiant:

I invite each of you
as members of this gathering
to indicate your support for <u>Bride</u> and <u>Groom</u>
by answering "I will"
to the following question:

By God's grace,
will each of you
do everything you can
to uphold and care for these two persons
in their marriage?

Guests: I will.

Marriage Address

A true marriage
is the ultimate relationship
because it offers the opportunity
of limitless intimacy
between two people.
It is a great and challenging adventure
into the depths and heights
of human caring, affection,
trust, and understanding.

For those who take its sacred vows,
their lives are intermingled
as the waters of two streams become one,
flowing together into a mighty river.

A true spiritual marriage
is a journey of transformation
into the profound mysteries
of life and creation.
In marriage, two become one,
and that one is far more complex and dynamic
than the simple addition of the two.

In marriage,
we do not give ourselves to another,
but rather surrender into something greater
while maintaining our balance
and well-being as individuals.
Together, we co-create a shared identity we call "we."

The Wedding Ceremony Planner

A truly sacred marriage union
is a vehicle for self-realization
that allows us to know our true selves
by reflection through our loved one.
Thus, marriage is a divine instrument
through which we come to know God's presence
in ourselves, in each other
and in the world around us.

<u>Bride</u> and <u>Groom</u>,
you have come here today
to surrender into the co-creation
of something wholly new and transcendent—
your precious, sacred, and unique marriage journey
as husband and wife.
Today, you step into
a much fuller experience and expression
of the mysteries and miracles of love.

Your precious, blessed, and sacred union
is lovely in its innocence,
mighty in its strength,
and abundant with possibilities.
It belongs to you both.
Over time you will give it an identity.
We wish for you the wisdom, strength of character,
and divine creativity
to make this a happy marriage,
a safe harbor,
and a joyful journey to share.

WATER CEREMONY

Many of us have been blessed to notice
that when we share
a true and abiding love with a partner,
even plain water tastes sweet.
<u>Bride</u> and <u>Groom</u>,
share this clear water now
as a symbol of the sweet and precious love you share.

(The Bride and Groom give each other a drink from the same glass.)

As you do so,
remember that just as you are now partaking
of the sweetness and purity
of this fresh and clean water,
you have already been blessed to partake
of the brilliance and magnificence
of the love you share.
By devoting yourselves
to cherishing and nurturing this love,
may your marriage grow sweeter
with each passing year.

WEDDING VOWS

Officiant:

<u>Bride</u> and <u>Groom</u>,
please join hands
and share your Wedding Vows.

Groom:

I, <u>Groom</u>, choose you, <u>Bride</u>,
as my life partner.
I am so glad

that I waited for my dreams to come true
because they did when I found you.
I am so blessed
that I get to be your partner
and am comforted to know
that I have chosen wisely.

Whatever life has in store for us,
I will honor and respect our marriage
and be by your side,
loving you through it all.
I will always strive
to be the husband of your dreams.
<u>Bride</u>, I will love you forever.

Bride:

I, <u>Bride</u>, promise to always keep my love for you alive
and out in front of all I do.
I promise to be faithful and true
no matter what challenges may come our way.
I promise to nurture you as my husband,
my lover, and my best friend.
I will continue to love you and cherish you,
walking through this life, together,
hand in hand.

RING EXCHANGE

Officiant:

May I have the rings, please?

Wedding rings are symbolic reminders
of the unbroken circle
of a healthy and abiding love.

Within the safety and comfort of a true marriage,
love freely given
has no beginning and no end.
Love freely given
has no separate giver and receiver.
Each of you gives your love to the other
and each of you receives love from the other
and the circle of love goes around and around.

May these rings serve to remind you
of the freedom and the power of your love.

The wedding ring is a circle
symbolizing the sun, and the earth,
and the universe.
It is a symbol of wholeness,
perfection, and peace.
As you enter into the circle
of your shared love,
may you be blessed
through your devotion to this union.
May your journey as husband and wife
be filled with peace and love and joy.

<u>Groom</u>, place this ring on <u>Bride</u>'s finger.

Groom:
　　With this ring,
　　I give you my promise
　　to honor you,
　　to be faithful to you,
　　and to share my love and my life with you
　　in all ways, always.

Officiant:

Bride, place this ring on Groom's finger.

Bride:

With this ring,
I give you my promise
to honor you,
to be faithful to you,
and to share my love
and my life with you
in all ways, always.

FINAL BLESSING AND PRONOUNCEMENT

Bride and Groom,
on behalf of your loved ones
who are here with you today,
I would like to mention some of the things
we wish for you:

First, we wish for you a love
that is rich and deep,
and powerful enough to inspire others
and to support you both
in bringing forth the best that is within you.
May you lavishly love one another
and love being loved by one another
today, tomorrow, and always.

Second, we wish for you the kind of home
that will be a sanctuary for you both,
a place of peace, freedom, vitality,
growth, and humor.
And in this home,

we hope that you are blessed
with a healthy and happy family.

Finally, we wish that at the end of your lives
you will be able to look back and smile
upon the life that you have shared together,
pleased, satisfied, and fulfilled
beyond your wildest dreams.

And now,
by the power vested in me by the State of ____,
it is my great pleasure
to pronounce you husband and wife.

Mr. and Mrs. ____,
you may now kiss as husband and wife
for the first time.
Congratulations and God bless you!

Ceremony Four: Inspired by Nature—Text Worksheet

Gathering Words:
#20, pages 98–99

Declaration of Support:
#4, pages 120–123; #5, paragraphs 1 and 2, page 123

Marriage Address:
#4, pages 131–132

Water Ceremony:
#1, pages 150–151

Wedding Vows:
   Groom: #8, page 159
   Bride: #13, page 160

Ring Exchange:
   Prelude #3, page 195; #10, page 198
   Ring Exchange #3, page 200

Final Blessing:
#3, pages 205–206

Ceremony Five:
Short, Spontaneous, and Intimate

This ceremony is one of the shortest and most intimate ones I have yet performed. It has no script, because that was one of the requirements of this particular couple. They wanted every word to be an authentic and spontaneous expression.

There were fifteen guests, including only their closest family members and friends. Before the ceremony, which took place in the backyard of the home they would share together, the guests mingled about until I gave them the sign that the ceremony was to begin. We all followed the Bride and Groom and processed to the spot where the ceremony was to take place. There was no music, except the sounds of nature—wind in the trees and a babbling brook nearby. We formed a circle, joined hands, and stood silently in this peaceful setting, bringing our focus together in loving harmony.

After a few moments of silence, long enough to move past the initial discomfort of this unfamiliar happening, I invited the guests to share their thoughts and feelings about the day. One by one, they all spoke and we laughed and cried together over the joy and tenderness of the bond among them all. Some of them shared stories—both hilarious and tender—about the Bride and Groom. Others simply expressed their best wishes and blessings for the couple.

After the last of us spoke, the Bride and Groom turned to each other and exchanged their wedding vows and rings as the final sharing. We all fell into a natural silence for a few moments. And, finally, I spoke. As previously arranged with the couple, I said, "I joyously affirm your union as wife and husband."

Ceremony Six:
A Marriage with Children

OPENING PRAYER

Beloved God,
we are gathered here,
uniting our hearts as one
in support and celebration of <u>Bride</u> and <u>Groom</u>
as they enter into the sacred and joyous covenant of marriage.

We ask you to bless the family
created by this union
as <u>Bride</u>'s daughter, <u>Child 1</u>,
and <u>Groom</u>'s son, <u>Child 2</u>,
join with them in the creation of a new family.

We ask that you guide and bless each of them
in loving and honoring one another
and in building and strengthening a family unit
that will be a safe and nurturing haven for them all.
Help them to find the balance and harmony
of their individuality and their shared life.

We ask that your light and grace
be extended to each of them,
that they may know you
and welcome you in their lives
each and every day.

THE UNITING OF FAMILIES AND FRIENDS

When a man and a woman come together in marriage,
their families and friends are also joined together
into a larger circle of caring.
From now on, you will know <u>Bride</u> and <u>Groom</u>
not only as individuals,
but as marriage partners,
and your individual lives will be linked together
as members of this community.

<u>Bride</u> and <u>Groom</u>,
today we have come together to celebrate
the love you have found with each other.
By being here with you,
each of us is declaring our support
for your decision to join together in marriage.

(To guests)

As families and friends,
you form the community of support
that surrounds <u>Bride</u> and <u>Groom</u>.
Each of you, by your presence here today,
is being called upon to uphold them
in honoring and loving each other.

Always stand beside them,
never between them.
Offer them your love and support,
not your judgment.
Encourage them with your kindness and loving hearts,
and honor this marriage
into which they have come to be joined today.

MARRIAGE ADDRESS

<u>Bride</u> and <u>Groom</u>,
you began as best friends,
and now that friendship has grown
into a loving and abiding commitment.

Remember that the strength and power
of the love you share with each other
and with your children
stand upon your health and well-being
as individuals.

In order to teach each other
how to love and care for you,
you will need to be aware
of your own needs as individuals
and lovingly communicate them to each other.

Tenderly nurture your children
so that they always feel your love
and know that they are safe and cared for.

Celebrate your love for each other
and for the children
each and every day.
Remember that God's infinite wisdom
brought you together
and will continue to light your path
all the days of your lives.

Share the gifts of your friendship,
your patience, and your tenderness.

Always nurture this partnership
with your incredible ability
to communicate with each other,
and your abiding respect for each other's strength,
wisdom, freedom and differences.

Continue to bless each other
with your eternal honesty
and your delight and gratitude
for the glory of being able to share your destiny.

Remember to let your children know
each and every day
how precious they are to you.
Surround each other and your children
with your tender loving care.

I wish you the courage
to keep your loving hearts open to each other
for the rest of your lives.

God bless you.

MARRIAGE VOWS AND RING EXCHANGE

Groom:

<u>Bride</u>, I have never known
the desire and passion you have created in me.
I never imagined these feelings were even possible.
Words cannot describe
our spiritual, physical, and emotional connection.
Life is a series of events and experiences
that together make us who we are;

that person someone else sees
when they meet you.

Bride, from the moment we met,
I discovered a unique bond
with a truly special person.
My life was forever changed,
and now, with you in my life,
each day is truly a lovely day.

We came together from separate paths
and today begin our journey along the same road,
our destinies forever linked,
our lives intertwined.

I have heard that love consists
not of gazing into each other's eyes,
but of looking outward together
in the same direction.
From deep within my heart,
I love you.

Bride, in you I have found someone to share
not only the good times, but the bad;
not only the pleasure, but the pain;
someone to support and be supported by.
You are my companion to confide in and console.
You are my best friend.

I am confident that with you,
none of life's obstacles will stand in our way
and together we will enjoy all that life has to offer.

<u>Bride</u>, my Love, my soul mate,
my partner, my best friend,
today I ask you to be my wife and companion.
I commit myself to you
for the rest of our lives together and beyond.
Please share with me the joy of guiding my son, <u>Child 2</u>,
as I will enjoy guiding your daughter, <u>Child 1</u>,
together raising our family.

Who knows what other beautiful facets
our relationship will foster.
For there awaits us all
the pleasure of growing together
in a life shared for years to come.

Bride:
Our love developed over time,
with respect for each other's talent and ability,
into a friendship.

As we supported and guided each other,
you patiently and tenderly broke down my walls.
While you taught me to look
into my heart and soul,
we shared our dreams, hopes,
fears, and desires.

Somewhere, probably sooner than either of us knew,
we fell in love.
I asked you to catch me while I was falling,
and you wrapped your loving arms around me.
<u>Groom</u>, as I gaze into your beautiful green eyes,

I look into your soul
and I join you there.

I have fallen in love with you, my best friend,
a thousand times.
I will fall in love with you thousands more,
giving my love to you freely.

Groom, I know that we will be tested
by the routines of daily life,
by chance and circumstance,
and by the full cycle of the seasons of life.
I am entering into our marriage
knowing that together
we will face life's sorrow
no less than its sweetness,
its frustration along with its grace and ease,
its disappointments along with its fulfillment.
I promise that, as your partner,
I will do my best
to help us keep our hearts open to each other
and the love flowing between us
even at the times this may be hardest to do.

I will remain at your side,
holding you close
and supporting you above all.

The strength of the connection we have between us
was evident when we first met.
In our lives,
I will continue to explore and develop that connection.

As I give myself to you in marriage,
I vow to be a loving woman,
filled with passion and friendship,
and to make a happy home
for both of us and our children.

When we are apart,
I will always look at the sky and the moon,
knowing that we are together,
never truly apart,
for our hearts and souls are so incredibly linked.

You have freed my wings for flying,
and I will fly with you forever.
I will look for your secret places
and share mine with you,
always working to keep our love new,
exciting, adventurous, and young,
especially as it grows in maturity and familiarity.

You were made to love me
and I was made to love you.
Our destinies intertwined,
bringing us together here today
and for the rest of our lives.
Keep your loving arms around me.
Our love proves to me
that fairy tales really do come true.
It will last forever.

We have reached our island!
Love...We are there!

Vows to the Children

Officiant:

> Bride, Groom, Child 1, and Child 2,
> you have all pledged your love to your new family
> and promised to love and nurture each other.
>
> Love is something very magical.
> It is a gift from God
> that lights us up inside.
> And when a man and a woman
> join their hearts together in marriage,
> their lights flow together
> and a single brighter light
> goes forth from their united being.
>
> When a family is formed as an extension of this union,
> the light is intensified
> by the light that flows from the children as well.
> The happiness you feel in being a family together
> is a reflection of this.
> This light that you have,
> this happiness,
> comes from God.
> So when we love one another,
> we are experiencing God's presence in our lives.
>
> Bride, Groom, Child 1, and Child 2,
> you are divine and eternal beings,
> and as you come to know this,
> you will never cease to wonder and glory
> in your coming together as a family.

By being a loving family,
you will awaken your love for God
and your knowledge of the fact
that within each human being
burns the spark of the divine.

When people love one another
with devotion and freedom,
they kindle the awareness
of that spark in each other
as nothing else quite can do.

<u>Bride</u>, <u>Groom</u>, <u>Child 1</u>, and <u>Child 2</u>,
in joining together today,
you kindle one another's divine light
and promise always to do your best
to see that light in each other
and to nurture and tend that divine flame
in one another
as best you can each day,
especially at the times it may be hardest to do,
and the times
when one of you may doubt or forget
the existence of that light
within yourself.

This ceremony marks not only the union of <u>Bride</u> and <u>Groom</u>
as husband and wife,
it also celebrates their joining together
with <u>Child 1</u> and <u>Child 2</u>
to form a new family.

Bride and Groom to Children:
(reading alternating paragraphs)

> <u>Child 1</u> and <u>Child 2</u>,
> we are now one family,
> a mom and dad, brother and sister.
> Each of you has so much beauty inside.
> You can do anything you choose to do with your life.
>
> We promise to be patient
> and to support each of you,
> to give you strength and room to grow,
> to do less correcting and more connecting,
> to stop playing serious and to seriously play,
> to do less tugging and do more hugging.
>
> Life is full of surprises,
> and we want you to know
> that no matter what happens,
> no matter what you do
> or who you become,
> we will always love you.
>
> <u>Child 1</u> and <u>Child 2</u>,
> today we give you these rings
> to remind you of our love
> and to serve as a symbol
> of the unity of our new family.

CHILDREN'S VOWS

Officiant:

> An absolute requirement in a wedding ceremony
> is the sharing before witnesses
> of vows between husband and wife.

The exchange of these vows
represents the moment of covenant between the two.
It is the vows which bind husband and wife
both spiritually and emotionally.
Vows are love made tangible
as they reach from and speak to the heart.

In creating today's ceremony,
<u>Child 1</u> and <u>Child 2</u> asked
if they could also take vows
to express their love and commitment to their new family.

It is true, <u>Child 1</u> and <u>Child 2</u>,
that something very special is happening
for you as well today.
In this ceremony,
you are sharing in the celebration
of the happiness that is present in your family,
and you are affirming your role
in that most fundamental of all human relationships.
May the joy and excitement of today
and the warmth and loving of your home
also serve as a model for you
of what you will seek and find
when it is your time to enter into marriage
and to create your own family.

<u>Child 1</u>, please repeat after me:
I, <u>Child 1</u>, do hereby promise
to love, honor, and cherish my family and God,
to always be honest and true about who I am,
and to honor and respect the truth
of each member of this family.

<u>Child 2</u>, please repeat after me:
I, <u>Child 2</u>, do hereby promise
to love, honor, and cherish my family and God,
to always be honest and true about who I am,
and to honor and respect the truth
of each member of this family.

FINAL BLESSING

<u>Bride</u> and <u>Groom</u>,
I wish you the courage
to keep your loving hearts open to each other
for the rest of your lives,
and to cherish the precious love you share.
May you continue to find delight in each other
and in your being together.
May your love forever nourish you
and keep you strong.

<u>Child 1</u> and <u>Child 2</u>,
may you also find the strength,
comfort, and support you need
as you grow and develop
as members of this family.

I wish you all the strength
to be true to the vows you have made here today.
May you always have the wisdom
to cherish the precious love you share.

May you abide by the laws of Spirit,
nurturing yourselves and each other
with acceptance, understanding,
cooperation, and loving.

May your home provide each of you as individuals,
and all of you as a family,
with a place of peace and health,
filled with blessings and joy.

<u>Bride</u> and <u>Groom</u>,
by the power vested in me by the State of ____,
I witness and affirm your union of love
and now pronounce you husband and wife.

You may now kiss as husband and wife for the first time.
Congratulations and God bless you!

(The children recess with their parents.)

Opening Prayer:
#9, pages 81–82

Uniting of Family and Friends:
Declaration of Support #3, paragraph 1, page 118; #1, page 117

Marriage Address:
#7, pages 134–135

Wedding Vows:
#40, pages 182–186

Vows to the Children:
Involving Children #5, pages 226–227; #2 (adapted for two children), page 222

Children's Vows:
Involving Children #4, pages 224–225

Final Blessing:
#7, paragraph 1, page 208; *#1; paragraphs 2–4, pages 203–204

*Adapted to include children

Ceremony Seven: Nondenominational Christian with Scriptural Readings

(After they process into the church, and before they take their seats, the parents of the Bride and Groom light two candles on either side of the Unity Candle to represent their families.)

SCRIPTURE READINGS

Officiant:

A reading from John 2, verses 1–11:

On the third day
there was a wedding in Cana in Galilee,
and the mother of Jesus was there:
Jesus also was invited to the wedding,
with his disciples.

When the wine ran out,
the mother of Jesus said to him,
"They have no wine."
And Jesus said to her,
"O woman, what does this have to do with me?
My hour has not yet come."
His mother said to the servants,
"Do whatever he tells you."

Now there were six stone water jars there,
for the Jewish rites of purification,
each holding twenty or thirty gallons.

Jesus said to the servants,
"Fill the jars with water."
And they filled them up to the brim.
And he said to them,
"Now draw some out,
and take it to the master of the feast."
So they took it.

When the master of the feast tasted the water
now become wine,
and did not know where it came from
(though the servants who had drawn the water knew),
the master of the feast called the Bridegroom
and said to him,
"Everyone serves the good wine first;
and when people have drunk freely,
then the poor wine;
but you have kept the good wine until now."

This, the first of his signs,
Jesus did at Cana in Galilee,
and manifested his glory;
and his disciples believed in him.

In Matthew, chapter 18, verse 20, Jesus says:

"Where two or three are gathered together
in my name,
there am I in the midst of them."

As represented here today,
in this union of <u>Bride</u> and <u>Groom</u>,
Christ is among us.

It is through their love
and among those who have gathered here today
to witness this union,
that our loving God reveals himself to us.

When we come together in God's name,
we put down our petty and powerful weapons
of judgment and rejection,
and all the ways that we have learned
to withhold ourselves from one another
and we reach together
into that which patiently awaits our choice
to turn away from the multitude of our illusions—
to the presence of God.
To truly enter into this presence,
we need to choose our oneness
rather than our separateness.

Christ taught us that the pathway
into the glory of our true selves
is through our loving hearts.
And it is through choosing our loving
that we truly worship God.

Our greatest blessing in life
comes not from power or possessions
but from the intimate knowing
and loving of another.
<u>Bride</u> and <u>Groom</u> are so blessed.

So, today is a celebration of their love
and how this love
brings God's presence into their lives,

for indeed,
a true marriage such as this one
is the highest form of knowing
and worshiping the Beloved.

MARRIAGE ADDRESS

<u>Bride</u> and <u>Groom</u>,
this bond you share is a true miracle
and a blessing from God.
Treasure it and carefully tend it each day.
You breathe life into each other
and provide a safe and sacred harbor
where you are able to shed
all of your worldly illusions
while witnessing, receiving, and cherishing
the precious truth of one another.
Generously shower each other
with the gifts of your faith, strength,
honesty, beauty, and complexity.

In the hardest of times,
always remember to reach for the Godness—
the goodness inside of yourselves and each other—
to the Oneness of our Lord's most loving message of
"When two or more are gathered in my name,
there I am also."

May you always honor the sanctity of your union
and thus be blessed
beyond your wildest dreams.

God bless you.

READING

Now, <u>Groom</u>'s sister, _____, will share a reading
from the first letter of John,
chapter 4, verses 7–16,
followed by an excerpt
from First Corinthians, chapter 13.

Dear friends,
let us love one another,
for love comes from God.
Everyone who loves
has been born of God
and knows God.

Whoever does not love
does not know God,
because God is love.

This is how God showed his love among us:
He sent his one and only Son
into the world
that we might live through him.

This is love:
not that we loved God,
but that he loved us
and sent his Son
as an atoning sacrifice for our sins.

Dear friends,
since God so loved us,
we also ought to love one another.

No one has ever seen God;
but if we love one another,
God lives in us
and his love is made complete in us.

We know that we live in him
and he in us,
because he has given us of his Spirit.

And we have seen and testify
that the Father has sent his Son
to be the Savior of the world.

If anyone acknowledges
that Jesus is the Son of God,
God lives in him
and he in God.

And so we know and rely on
the love God has for us.
God is love.
Whoever lives in love
lives in God,
and God in him.

Love is patient, love is kind.
It does not envy, it does not boast,
it is not proud.

It is not rude, it is not self-seeking,
it is not easily angered,
it keeps no record of wrongs.

Love does not delight in evil,
but rejoices with the truth.

It always protects, always trusts,
always hopes, always perseveres.

Love never fails.

CANDLE CEREMONY

Officiant:
> The lighting of the Unity Candle is a ritual
> symbolizing the union of a man and a woman
> as they enter into marriage.
> The Unity Candle itself represents the oneness
> that is being created by the joining of their individual lives
> into a shared journey.
> The individual candles
> symbolize the uniqueness of <u>Bride</u> and <u>Groom</u>
> as they walk side by side
> heading in the same direction.
> They are separate, yet one.
>
> The lighting of the Unity Candle
> in the presence of God
> symbolizes the great mystery
> of the union of two becoming one.
> <u>Bride</u> and <u>Groom</u>, always remember
> that as you join together in marriage,
> you are still two separate beings,
> each with your own unique needs, dreams, and desires,
> and that in marriage,
> you are creating a covenant
> of loving, caring, and sharing between you.

Now, <u>Bride</u> and <u>Groom</u>,
as you bring these lights
which symbolize your individual selves
closer and closer together,
your flames merge into the greater light of your union.

As you light the Unity Candle
to symbolize the enduring flame of your marriage,
let us each take a moment
to silently express our prayerful wishes
for your happiness and well-being
in this marriage.
And let us remember
that just as <u>Bride</u> and <u>Groom</u> are becoming one,
so are we coming together
into a circle of family and friends
in loving support of this marriage.

<u>Bride</u> and <u>Groom</u>,
tend the light of your loving union
with great devotion and kindness.
May you be blessed
with a lifelong partnership
of loving and learning through God's grace.

Wedding Vows

Please join hands and share your Wedding Vows.

Groom:

In the name of God,
I, ___, take you, ___,
to be my wife.

It is you, above all others,
who has awakened my soul
and enthused me with the possibility
of becoming all that I am capable of being
in this world.
I am so grateful to you for these blessings.

I want you to know
how much I cherish your friendship
and how much I appreciate your belief in me.
Your love is my greatest treasure.

I will be at your side
through all of life's challenges and joys
as we become one in spirit before God.
I promise to give of myself to you
in every way I can,
to care for you and protect you
as I would my own self.
I promise to be faithful to you in this life,
and to be honest and true to our union
until God, in his perfect wisdom and timing,
calls one of us to death.

Bride, I promise
to carry the flame of your love with me forever
in this world and the next,
so that the light of our love,
now one light
drawn from the mingling of two souls,
will always prevail.

Bride, I will forever thank God
for your presence in my life
and you will always be surrounded by my love.

May God always keep us
and watch over our love and our home.

Bride:
Groom, I strongly believe
that our union is God's will.
Therefore, through his grace,
I, Bride, take you, Groom,
to be my beloved husband.
And, with all the sincerity in my heart,
I promise to love you dearly,
to confide in you honestly,
to respect you proudly,
and to always be kind.

I have learned, through you,
the importance of being true to myself,
and as your partner,
I will strive to be fair and true to you.

I look forward to our life together,
enriched by our friendship
and the encouragement we give to one another.
And I am comforted to know
you have promised to be by my side
in times of fear and sorrow.

<u>Groom</u>, from this moment forward,
I offer to you all that I am
and all that I hope to be.
I will be faithful to you
and grateful to God for our love
all the days of my life.

RING EXCHANGE
Officiant:
May I have the rings, please?

Let us pray.

Bless, O Lord, the giving of these rings,
that they who wear them
may abide in thy peace
and continue in thy favor;
through Jesus Christ our Lord.

May <u>Bride</u> and <u>Groom</u> abide in thy peace
and grow in their knowledge of your presence
through their loving union.
May the seamless circle of these rings
become the symbol of their endless love
and serve to remind them of the covenant
they have entered into today
to be faithful, loving, and kind to each other.

Beloved God,
may they abide in your grace
and be forever true to this union.

Amen.

<u>Groom</u>, place this ring on <u>Bride</u>'s finger.

Groom:
> <u>Bride</u>, I give you this ring
> in token and pledge
> of my abiding love for you.
>
> <u>Bride</u>, with this ring,
> I thee wed,
> in the name of the Father,
> and the Son,
> and the Holy Spirit.
> Amen.

Officiant:
> <u>Bride</u>, place this ring on <u>Groom</u>'s finger.

Bride:
> <u>Groom</u>, I give you this ring
> in token and pledge
> of my abiding love for you.
>
> <u>Groom</u>, with this ring,
> I thee wed,
> in the name of the Father,
> and the Son,
> and the Holy Spirit.
> Amen.

MUSICAL INTERLUDE
"Ave Maria"

THE PRONOUNCEMENT OF MARRIAGE

Officiant:

Beloved Father, Mother, God,
we ask you to bless <u>Bride</u> and <u>Groom</u>
with the strength to keep the vows they have made,
and to cherish the love they share,
that they may be faithful and devoted to each other.
Help them to support each other
with patience, understanding, and honesty.
Enable them to have a home
that is a place of blessings and of peace.

We seek your love and grace
for all who are witnesses of this holy marriage.
May all who share the marriage covenant be renewed
through their witnessing this union.

<u>Bride</u> and <u>Groom</u>,
may your life together be joyful;
may you both be enriched
and made better people
for living in this blessed union.
May the grace and wisdom of God
be always with you.
May the love of God always fill you,
surround you, and protect you.
Amen.

Now, because you have chosen one another
and pledged to love each other
for all the days of your lives,
before God
and before this loving community of family and friends,
it gives me great joy
to pronounce you husband and wife.

You may now kiss.

BENEDICTION
Beloved God,
source of love and light and sound,
pour your grace down upon <u>Bride</u> and <u>Groom</u>,
that they may fulfill the vows
that they have made today
through their love and faithfulness to each other.

<u>Bride</u> and <u>Groom</u>,
go in peace and love,
seeing in each other
the face of God smiling upon you
and blessing you each and every day.

(Parents light two candles on either side of the Unity Candle to represent the families of the Bride and Groom.)

Scriptural Readings:
John 2:1–11; Matthew 18:20

Marriage Address:
#6, pages 133–134; #2, paragraphs 5 and 6, page 129

Readings:
First John, Chapter 4:7–16, Groom's sister _____
First Corinthians, Chapter 13:4–8, Groom's sister _____

Candle Ceremony:
#5, page 146

Wedding Vows:
Groom: #2, paragraph 1, page 156; #37, pages 178–179; #25, paragraph 5, page 168; #9, last line, page 159
Bride: #41, page 187

Ring Exchange:
Prelude #4 and #5 combined, pages 195–196
Ring Exchange #2, page 198

Musical Interlude:
"Ave Maria" (by string quartet)

Final Blessing:
#2 (omit last line), page 205; #6, pages 207–208

Benediction:
#6, page 210

Ceremony Eight:
Joyful Family Togetherness

GATHERING WORDS

For those of us blessed by a true partnership of love,
we feel safe in the presence of our loved one.
There is no need to hide any part of ourselves
for fear of being judged or rejected.
We can just be together from moment to moment,
believing that those moments
will thread together into eternity.

There is a gentleness to the presence of love
that softens life's rough edges.
It makes us somehow braver
to go forth into the world
knowing that the shelter of someone's love
awaits us at day's end.

We are most vulnerable when we love.
We place our trust in another
to honor us and to care for us,
to treasure us and to receive our love.

In love, we trust
that the other will provide a safe haven
in which we can experience and share
the fullness of our being with one another.
And in so doing, we trust
that our lives will be far richer

than had we chosen separate journeys
through this world.

We trust that our love will fill us full
and make us wiser and more beautiful beings.
We find that our union graces our lives with balance,
a sweetness beyond any we have ever tasted,
and a treasure beyond any measure of value
we have ever known.

Whenever we attend a wedding celebration,
we are given the opportunity
to reexamine our own lives.
We might look at the radiance of the couple before us
and be tempted to compare their obvious joy
to the quality of our own primary relationships.

The truth is that each one of us is a powerful creator
in the dance of love and marriage.
Each one of us, each moment of every day,
has the choice to rededicate ourselves to one another
or to withhold our love and caring.

Love is powerful.
It is simple.
Yet it is very complex.

In order for love to flow between two people,
four things must be happening at once.
Each person gives their love to the other
and each is the receiver of the other's love.
Love requires us to be vulnerable to each other

so that our love may flow back and forth
through these four doors.

There are so many ways
that we can choose to be in relationship to each other.
It is only through love
that our spirits are lifted into a oneness
that transcends all the dualities
we experience in our lives.
Loving is the only experience that enables us to see
that our separation is only a condition
of the physical and material level of being—
that our souls can soar and merge as one.

It is love that gives the deepest meaning to our lives.
It is our highest calling,
our greatest purpose, and our finest achievement.

One of the great joys of the wedding day
is the joining together
of the couple's families and friends.
<u>Bride</u> and <u>Groom</u> are filled with gratitude
to each and every one of you
for the loving, caring, friendship, and support
that you have given them throughout their lives.

Being able to share their wedding day with you,
surrounded by your love and support,
is a treasured blessing.
Knowing that your best wishes go forward
with Bride and Groom
strengthens them as they embark upon their journey
as husband and wife.

A Letter Written and Read by Groom's Son

<u>Bride</u> and <u>Groom</u>,

I wish you every happiness on your wedding day.
May it exceed your wildest dreams
as a day filled with laughter, community, and fair skies,
perfectly lovely in every detail.

May this day live forever in your hearts
as the beautiful beginning of your forever together.
May the days that follow be a romantic, magical time,
discovering the joy of living together as one.

And as the days turn to weeks and months and years,
take the time to enjoy the little things in life,
like lavender sunsets and evening walks.

May you both wake each morning
to the happy surprise that you love one another
even more than the day before.
And may you gracefully learn life's lessons
of patience and compromise
as you learn to trust each other's feelings
as your own.

Your first year of marriage
will be gone before you know it.
Treasure each anniversary as a happy reminder
of the vows that join your hearts,
your minds, and your destinies.
Perhaps your favorite anniversary gift
will be to renew your vows each passing year.

May your days "for better,"
"for richer," and "in health"
far outnumber stormy days
and times of trouble.

As you live and love throughout the years,
may you realize all the fulfillment
marriage can bring,
and know that all your days have been happier
because you have shared them with each other.

MARRIAGE ADDRESS

Officiant:

Bride and Groom,
demonstrate your love for yourselves
and each other
through caring and sharing.
Stretch your love large enough
to embrace whatever life brings to you.
Let it fill you, surround you,
comfort and protect you.
Let your hearts be truly safe
and at home with each other.

Be generous in expressing your love.
Be open to receive love from each other.
Be flexible and forgiving with each other.
Let your relationship be a catalyst that transforms you
into the expression of your highest selves.

Remember that your relationship is alive
and ever-changing

and that your love is a miracle,
always inviting you to grow, to learn,
to blossom, and to expand.
How you regard each other
and how you behave toward each other
will determine the destiny of your union.
It is your creation together,
your sacred responsibility.
Be kind to your relationship.
Nourish it with tender loving care,
and, above all else,
keep your loving alive.
Treat it as the precious blessing it is.

Do not just be married or in love;
but let your marriage be an active process of
loving each other.

The quality of your marriage is up to you.
Both of you as individuals
and together as a couple
will choose what kind of marriage
you will create, promote, and allow
through your thoughts, feelings, and actions each day.

May you always honor the sanctity of your union
and thus be blessed beyond your wildest dreams.

WEDDING VOWS

Officiant:

    I now invite you all to join me
    in witnessing <u>Bride</u>'s and <u>Groom</u>'s Wedding Vows.

<u>Groom</u>, do you take this woman
as your wife and equal,
your lover and your best friend;
keeping yourself only unto her,
for as long as you both shall live?

Groom: Yes, I do.

Officiant:
<u>Bride</u>, do you take this man
as your husband and equal,
your lover and your best friend;
keeping yourself only unto him,
for as long as you both shall live?

Bride: Yes, I do.

RING EXCHANGE
Officiant:
May I have the rings, please?

These rings are circles,
and circles are symbolic of the sun,
the earth, and the universe.
As arms that embrace,
these wedding rings you give and receive this day
reflect the circle of shared love
into which you enter
as partners in life.

May you always be blessed,
and may you abide in peace and love.

<u>Groom</u>, place this ring on <u>Bride's</u> finger.

Groom:
    As a sign of my love
    and my knowledge that in marrying you,
    I am becoming much more than I am,
    I give you this ring
    with the promise
    that I will love you
    and keep my heart open to you
    all the days of my life.

Officiant:
    <u>Bride</u>, place this ring on <u>Groom</u>'s finger.

Bride:
    As a sign of my love
    and my knowledge that in marrying you,
    I am becoming much more than I am,
    I give you this ring
    with the promise
    that I will love you
    and keep my heart open to you
    all the days of my life.

FINAL BLESSING
    Now, because you have chosen one another
    and pledged to love each other
    for all the days of your lives,
    before God
    and before this loving community of family and friends,
    it gives me great joy

to pronounce you husband and wife.
Congratulations!

Mr. and Mrs. ____,
you may now kiss as husband and wife
for the first time!

Ceremony Eight: Joyful Family Togetherness—Text Worksheet

Gathering Words:
#3, pages 84–85; #4, pages 85–86; #14, pages 94–95

Reading:
A Letter written and read by the Groom's son

Marriage Address:
#2 (omit paragraph 5), pages 128–129

Wedding Vows:
#15, page 162

Ring Exchange:
    Prelude #2, page 195
    Ring Exchange #6, page 200

Final Blessing:
#6, pages 207–208

A Note about Commitment Ceremonies

Most people think of commitment ceremonies as being only for gay and lesbian couples, without realizing how many circumstances might bring a heterosexual couple to choose a nonlegal recognition of their union. For those who are either not legally qualified to marry or do not want a legal bond, the commitment ceremony is an appropriate solution not only for same-sex couples, but also for elderly couples who choose this approach for tax and inheritance reasons or other heterosexual couples whose circumstances somehow prevent them from legally marrying.

For these occasions, couples usually want much the same sentiment expressed as do couples who are becoming legally married. The following sample ceremony was performed for a couple mentioned earlier who could not be legally married because his divorce was not final. Since her father was dying, there was a sense of urgency to fulfill his dream of walking his daughter down the aisle. Some simple changes in phraseology met their needs quite nicely. For example, instead of referring to their "wedding day," we used terms like their "day of celebration" and referred to their "union" rather than to their "marriage." Instead of declaring them husband and wife, I declared them life partners.

The governing authorities for commitment ceremonies are the same as those for wedding ceremonies—the church and state in which the union is taking place. In any given state in the U.S., couples joined in commitment ceremonies may or may not have access to the same legal and social privileges as marriage partners. A number of religious denominations perform commitment ceremonies and couples can inquire among the clergy to find an appropriate Officiant. As with marriage ceremonies, each denomination has its own prescribed ceremonial format. This too will affect a couple's choice of where to declare their commitment.

Ceremony Nine:
A Heartfelt Commitment Ceremony

OPENING PRAYER

Let us begin by welcoming the presence of God
within each of us.

As we lift into the loving
that joins us together as one,
let us surround <u>Partner A</u> and <u>Partner B</u> with our love,
our prayers, and our best wishes for them
on this day of celebration
and throughout their journey together
as life partners.

We are here because we love <u>Partner A</u> and <u>Partner B</u>.
We rejoice that they have found each other
and that through each other,
they have come to know the power of love
as they have never known it before.

We celebrate this union
of their hearts, minds, bodies, and souls
and wish them great joy.

GATHERING WORDS

If you ask most couples
who have a strong and abiding love
what they like most about their partners,
usually they will say
that they don't have to pretend to be anything

other than what they are.
They are able to express themselves
without fear of being judged or rejected.
There is room in the relationship
for both of them to be unique individuals.
They are free to surrender
to the possibility of profound intimacy—
to be known and loved without condition.

For quite some time now,
<u>Partner A</u> and <u>Partner B</u> have known and loved each other.
They have been strengthened by their love
and have received many blessings
through its beauty and tenderness.
They have learned that they can depend on each other
and on the power of their love,
and that through each other
they are becoming better people.

Today, they come before us
to declare their commitment to each other
as life partners,
vowing to share the trials and triumphs
of their shared life.
They are declaring to each other
and to all of us present
that they will be by each other's side
no matter what life brings their way.

Love has gathered us here today.
We are here to celebrate the love
that <u>Partner A</u> and <u>Partner B</u> have for each other,
as well as the love that each of you has given them

throughout their lives.
As families and friends, you are the ones
who have taught <u>Partner A</u> and <u>Partner B</u> how to love.
You have shown them the blessings
that come through loving one another.

Having planted this seed of love in them,
we are now gathered to support them
as they embark upon their voyage of discovery
as life partners.
We are here to see them off on this journey.
Let us also be there to see them through.

FRIENDSHIP CIRCLE

<u>Partner A</u> and <u>Partner B</u> have expressed to me
the importance of actively involving all of you
in their celebration today.
So, we are going to share a ritual,
the Friendship Circle,
that originated in the Quaker tradition.

In a moment,
I'm going to ask you all to get up
and form a circle around the chairs.
Then, anyone who wishes to
may share their thoughts and feelings
about <u>Partner A</u> and <u>Partner B</u>
joining their lives together.
You may want to offer them your blessing
or to share a story about them,
or a reflection of a time
you have shared together.
Whatever comes forward is just fine.

So now, let us form our circle of family and friends.

(Everyone forms a circle and the Officiant invites guests to begin their sharing.)

CANDLE CEREMONY

This flame you ignite before us today
is strong and shining brightly.
May you tend it well
so that it may shine throughout your lives.

May the warmth of the love it symbolizes
forever bring you courage,
reassurance, and comfort
and fill you both with strength and joy.

COMMITMENT VOWS

Please join hands to share your vows.

Partner A:

I, Partner A, choose you, Partner B,
in the presence of our friends and families,
to be my partner from this time forward;
to love you,
to be a comfort and safe haven in your life,
to hold you close,
to listen deeply when you speak,
to nourish you with my gentleness,
to uphold you with my strength,
to weigh the effects of the words I speak
and the things I do,
to never take you for granted,

and to always give thanks
for your presence in my life.

Partner B:

Dearest <u>Partner A</u>,
I choose you to be my partner for life,
to be by your side
through our life's journey together.

You are my best friend.
You are my precious love.
You are the one I choose
to spend my life with.
I promise to cherish you, to honor you,
to love and respect you.
I promise to comfort and encourage you,
when we are healthy
and when we must endure sickness;
when we are filled with the joys of success
and when we are burdened with sorrows.

<u>Partner A</u>,
I promise to love you without condition
for all the days of my life.

RING EXCHANGE

Officiant:

May I have the rings, please?

These rings are a symbol
that has been carried forward from antiquity.

They are simple and strong.
They are round like the sun and the moon,
like the eye, and like the embrace of love.

As circles, rings remind us
that as we give our love,
so it comes back around to us,
and we give and receive love around and around
in the circle of love.

May your commitment rings
always serve as a reminder to you
that your love, like the sun and moon, illumines;
that your love, like the eye, lets you see clearly;
and your love, like an embrace,
is a grace upon this world.

Partner A, place this ring on Partner B's finger.

Partner A:
Partner B, with this ring
I am giving you my promise
to always love you,
cherish you,
honor you,
and comfort you.
I will always be grateful to God
for your presence in my life.

Officiant:

Partner B, place this ring on Partner A's finger.

Partner B:

Partner A, from the moment we met,
I knew I wanted to spend my life with you.
With this ring, I pledge myself to you,
to our union,
and to our everlasting love.

FINAL BLESSING
Officiant:

Now that Partner A and Partner B
have joined themselves to each other by solemn vows,
and by the giving and receiving of rings,
I pronounce that they are partners for life.
Congratulations and God bless you!

Ceremony Nine: A Heartfelt Commitment* Ceremony— Text Worksheet

Opening Prayer:
#1, page 75; #3, paragraphs 2 and 3, page 76

Gathering Words:
#5, page 86; #6, page 87; #7, pages 87–88

Friendship Circle:
#1, page 219

Candle Ceremony:
#7, pages 148–149

Wedding Vows:
Partner A: #5, page 157
Partner B: #6, pages 157–158

Ring Exchange:
Prelude #9, page 198
Ring Exchange: Partner A: #7, page 201
Ring Exchange: Partner B: #8, page 201

Final Blessing:
#5, page 207

*Text has been modified to create a commitment ceremony rather than a wedding ceremony.

Ceremony Ten:
Renewal of Marriage Vows

Some couples like to publicly renew their commitment to each other and celebrate the achievement of their lasting marriage. Typically, a vow renewal ceremony is held on the couple's wedding anniversary date. Following is a marriage renewal ceremony performed for a couple who had been married for twenty-five years and now had three sons. They had a copy of their original ceremony, which we referenced in the renewal service. Thus, their original wedding ceremony text has been blended together with material from this book.

GATHERING WORDS

We are gathered here together as families and friends
to celebrate the fact that <u>Wife</u> and <u>Husband</u>
have shared twenty-five years of marriage together.

For better, for worse,
for richer, for poorer,
in sickness, and in health,
they have found the strength in their love and commitment
to endure and to enjoy all that has come their way.

They have not only shared a marriage,
but have raised three sons as well:
<u>Son 1</u>, <u>Son 2</u>, and <u>Son 3</u>.
They have formed a family of individuals
who love and care for each other
and who can count on each other

to be there for one another.
So, <u>Wife</u>, <u>Husband</u>,
and <u>Son 1</u>, <u>Son2</u>, and <u>Son 3</u>,
today we celebrate you as a family as well.

<u>Wife</u> and <u>Husband</u>,
as Reverend _____ reminded you twenty-five years ago,
"Marriage and the union it symbolizes
can be the most sublime of human experiences;
for in any final accounting,
love is what life is all about."

Yet it was not that wedding ceremony that married you,
but rather your mutual commitment
to love and respect each other
in both the good times and the bad.

And so you stand before us today
with a seasoned love
that has been strengthened through the test of time.
You are still filled with hope and commitment,
and you are an inspiration to us all
as you recommit
to the sacred and joyous covenant
of your marriage here today.

Being here with <u>Wife</u> and <u>Husband</u>
serves as a reminder to us all
that the commitment of a man and a woman in marriage
is of the heart, body, mind, and spirit,
and is for the intention
of mutual love, help, and comfort
through the trials and triumphs of life.

It is a relationship
not to be entered into unadvisedly or lightly,
but deliberately, lovingly, and reverently.

As <u>Wife</u> and <u>Husband</u> have learned,
the choice to enter into marriage is profound.
In choosing a lifelong partner,
we are choosing the one
who will witness our changes and growth,
and who will affect these changes
and shape our maturation as well.

<u>Wife</u> and <u>Husband</u> have learned
through their years together
that the essence of a marriage relationship
is the openness to another person
in his or her entirety
as lover, companion, and friend.
They joined their lives together
in search of something greater and richer,
and created a life
that transcended their solitary paths.

They found that really loving one another
with depth and passion
is the greatest treasure.
It has added richness and profound meaning
to their lives.
They have discovered
that love is one of life's greatest joys.
By simply giving of themselves to each other,
honestly and courageously,
they have both been infinitely enhanced.

As companions in day-to-day life,
<u>Wife</u> and <u>Husband</u> have taken pleasure
in sharing their time
and thoughts and feelings.
They have delighted in reporting in
on their separate adventures in the world,
which have become the rhythm of life
between these devoted partners
as they have built their life together.

In this marriage, two lives are intimately shared;
and the blending of the two
has not diminished either one.
Rather, it has enhanced the individuality of each partner.

As this marriage has matured,
it has taken on a life of its own.
And within it,
<u>Wife</u> and <u>Husband</u> have individually evolved
while growing in understanding of each other.
This wonderful intimacy
has mirrored a depth of inner knowing
that has awakened levels of awareness
they never knew existed.
To be awakened in this way
is a priceless gift.

When we give of ourselves
into a loving marriage partnership,
we do not abandon ourselves;
we do not shed our individuality;
for that is what brought us together in the first place.

Each of us knows
that a marriage is not created by law or a ceremony;
but rather it occurs in the hearts of two human beings.
It grows out of loving, caring, and sharing
ourselves with each other.
And so it is that <u>Wife</u> and <u>Husband</u>
have connected their hearts and souls one to the other,
drawing upon the depths of their being,
into the deep well of human need—
the need to live united, and loving, and complete.

So, in witnessing this ceremony today,
we are observing only an outward sign
of an inward union
that exists between <u>Wife</u> and <u>Husband</u>.
Today, they have come before us
to publicly reaffirm their love;
to promise to continue to nurture themselves,
each other, and this union;
and to acknowledge its centrality in their lives.
They do so
knowing that marriage is at once
the most tender, yet challenging,
of all relations in life.

One of the great joys of this day
is the joining together
as a community of family and friends.
<u>Wife</u> and <u>Husband</u> are filled with gratitude
to each and every one of you
for the loving, caring, friendship, and support
that you have given them throughout their marriage.

Being able to share this day with you,
surrounded by your love and support,
is a treasured blessing.

CANDLE CEREMONY

Every human being possesses a special light
that burns within them.
When two spirits, destined to be together,
find each other,
their streams of light flow together,
and a single, brighter light
goes forth from their union.
When a family is formed
as an extension of this union,
the light is intensified
by the light that flows from the children, as well.
When people love one another
with devotion and freedom,
they kindle the awareness of that spark in each other
as nothing else quite can do.

Wife, Husband, and Son 1, Son 2, and Son 3,
in your commitment to one another,
you kindle one another's divine light,
and promise always to do your best
to see that light in each other;
to nurture and tend that spirit in one another
as best you can,
especially in difficult times,
when it may be hardest to do,
and the times when one of you may doubt or forget
the existence of that light within one another.

<u>Wife</u>, <u>Husband</u>, and <u>Son 1</u>, <u>Son 2</u>, and <u>Son 3</u>,
take these candles now,
and as you light them,
symbolically enter the sacred trust
to honor the divine spirit in one another.

Now, bring your individual flames together,
symbolizing the new and greater flame of your family,
remembering that just as this union is made stronger
by your strength as individuals,
so are you as individuals
made stronger by the strength of this union.

Renewal of Vows and Ring Exchange

<u>Wife</u> and <u>Husband</u>,
please join hands to renew your marriage vows.

You have traveled a long way together
to reach this place today.
In rededicating yourselves to each other,
this marriage, and your family,
you are affirming that:
    You are friends and choose to remain so.
    You are lovers and choose to remain so.
    You are individuals and choose to remain so.
    And you are partners and choose to remain so.

<u>Wife</u> and <u>Husband</u>,
as you place these rings on each other's fingers,
please reaffirm your marriage vows.

Husband:

> Wife, I feel blessed to have found you as my partner
> and I look forward to sharing the rest of my life with you.

Wife:

> Husband, I feel blessed to have found you as my partner
> and look forward to sharing the rest of my life with you.

FINAL BLESSING

Officiant:

> Wife and Husband,
> twenty-five years ago you entered this marriage
> with hope, commitment, and a newfound love.
> Today, you stand before us
> reaffirming a commitment
> that has stood the test of time,
> that has strengthened you as individuals,
> and taught you about the power of love in your lives.
> It is an honor and a blessing
> for each of us to be here with you today,
> celebrating your love and commitment
> to each other and to your family.
>
> May you continue to find delight in each other,
> and may your love continue to grow
> and to nurture you
> all the days of your lives.
>
> I wish you the strength
> to continue to keep the vows you have made
> and the good fortune

to find ever greater tenderness,
joy, and comfort
in the love you share.
Support each other, your marriage, and family
with patience, understanding, and honesty.

May your home continue to be
a place of peace and health,
filled with blessings and joy.

May you endlessly delight one another.
May you love and fulfill each other always.
Go in peace.
Live in joy.
Thanks be to God.
Congratulations and God bless you!

You may now kiss!

This ceremony blends together elements from the couple's original marriage ceremony with excerpts from this book. Listed below are the passages that have been adapted for inclusion in this ceremony:

Gathering Words:
#9, alternate paragraph 1, page 89; #10, paragraph 2, page 90; #11, paragraphs 2–7, pages 90–91; #17, paragraphs 3 and 4, page 97; #14, pages 94–95

Candle Ceremony:
#2, pages 141–142

Renewal of Vows and Ring Exchange:
Customized

Final Blessing:
#1, pages 203–204

Benediction:
#2, page 209

8

Checklists and Worksheets

In this section, you will find blank copies of the sample checklists and worksheets found in this book. They address both the design of your text and all elements of staging the ceremony. Below is a listing of each one, identifying where they can be found in the text as well as the page number of the blank copy on the following pages.

Ceremony Site Layout Worksheet

Describe exactly how the ceremony site will be set up, including the location of all flowers, decorations and props, Musicians, Readers, the Officiant, Wedding Party members, chairs, and so on. Describe them all in relationship to each other.

Chairs:

Flowers, Decorations and Props:

Officiant and Wedding Party:

Musicians:

Readers:

Photographer:

Other:

Wedding Day Information Sheet

Ceremony Location:
Rehearsal (Date and Time):
Ceremony (Date and Time):

Participants/Resources	Name	Phone	Email

Just Before the Ceremony Checklist

List everything that needs a final check to ensure that all goes smoothly.
Indicate who will check which items.

Activity	Person Responsible

Wedding Rehearsal Checklist

Prior to the Rehearsal, contact the Officiant and Location Coordinator to discuss who should attend the Rehearsal, who will be in charge, and what elements need to be rehearsed. List the sequence of Rehearsal events below.

Things I need to bring to my Rehearsal: (See sample worksheet on page 53.)

Designing the Ceremony Text Worksheet

Create a rough draft. Use the sample text elements that have been included in this book and any others that you have gathered for inclusion in your ceremony. For example, you may want to include a religious or family tradition. List all items in the order in which you would like them to occur. If you only want a segment of a sample item or want to change the wording, make note of that here as well. Remember, this is just a rough draft. So don't be too concerned about editing at this point. Just focus on gathering those elements that speak to you, at least in part. At this stage, you are likely to select more passages than will appear in your final ceremony text.

Opening Prayer:
Gathering Words:
Remembrances and Acknowledgments:
  Names to be included:
Readings and Songs:
  Selection:
  Author:
  Reader or Singer's Name:
Declaration of Support:
Marriage Address:
Sacred Rituals:
Wedding Vows:
  Groom:
  Bride:
Ring Exchange:
  Prelude:
  Ring Exchange:
Final Blessing:
Benediction:
Other:

Once you have created a rough draft according to your directions above, begin the editing and fine-tuning process. Be sure to read the text aloud to see that it flows smoothly and is not too long or short for what you want. Set a specific deadline for completing the ceremony text well in advance of the ceremony.

Processional Cues and Sequencing Worksheet

1. Describe what will happen prior to the Wedding Party processing. Include who will determine when to start and who will cue whom; if mothers, grandmothers, or other honored guests will be formally seated; how the music will be coordinated; and how the Officiant, Groom, and Groomsmen will take their places.

2. Describe the order in which the Wedding Party will walk up the aisle and where each one will go. If there is an aisle runner, who will attend to it and how will they be cued?

Recessional Cues and Sequencing Worksheet

Describe the sequencing of the Recessional and where each person will go once they are down the aisle. What will be the cue for the Musicians to begin playing? Will the parents follow the Wedding Party? Will there be a receiving line and, if so, where will it be and who will be in it? Who will be signing the marriage license, when and where will they meet the officiant?

A Note to Officiants

While this book is written primarily to assist couples who are seeking to design their own wedding ceremonies, it is also intended as a reference manual for those who officiate at wedding ceremonies. When I first started performing weddings, I found two books that showed me the way. But neither was really comprehensive in helping me address the myriad details and issues that I would face in years to come. My hope is that by sharing what I have learned, others will feel well supported.

There is something quite remarkable about having the "power" to declare a man and woman to be husband and wife or to officiate at a commitment ceremony where two people publicly declare their love and devotion to one another. Above and beyond this, officiating is a wonderful opportunity to be of service to couples by guiding them through the process of creating the ceremony that is right for them and that will set a good foundation for their marriage.

There is no question that many couples who are embarking on the process of designing their own wedding ceremony are in need of reliable guidance. While time and other considerations can cause us as officiants to place what seem like reasonable limits on our responsibilities to couples, we must not forget that their need provides us with the privilege to be of service in an enormously meaningful way. It is up to each of us to decide the degree to which we are willing to go above and beyond the call of duty to serve them. Just remember, as with any act of true service, it is the one who serves who reaps the richest rewards.

Here are some suggestions for ways to assist couples:

1. Keep a list of books and reference materials that you find particularly useful. If you are so inclined, maintain a lending library of these materials.

2. Provide checklists and worksheets like the ones in this book. You might even customize your own to the specific locations where you perform ceremonies.

3. Have couples fill out the checklists and worksheets, then meet with them to help fine-tune the details.

4. Hold a clear intention of doing whatever you can to assist the couple in creating the ceremony that is right for them and ensuring that it runs smoothly.

5. If for some reason you cannot perform the wedding of a couple who comes to you, be prepared to give them some specific and constructive suggestions about how to find another Officiant.

For the benefit of those of you who are fairly new at officiating customized wedding ceremonies, I will share my own process of working with couples to give you a place to start as you evolve your own model. Typically, my first contact with a couple is a phone call or email in response to their having discovered me on the Internet, or having been referred to me by a Bridal Consultant or a Location Coordinator if their ceremony and reception are taking place at the same location. In the initial conversation I do the following:

- First, check to see if I am available for their wedding location, date, and time.
- Answer any immediate questions or concerns they have about their ceremony or about my ministry.

- Discuss my approach and fees.
- If appropriate, I schedule an appointment to meet for an hour. The purpose of that meeting is for the couple to determine if I am the right one to perform their ceremony.
- In order that the couple not feel pressured to make a decision during our meeting, I ask them to call me afterwards with their decision.
- Since most couples don't know how to evaluate Officiants, I ask them to discuss what is important to them in this regard before our meeting so they can be prepared with specific questions.

If the couple decides they would like me to perform their ceremony, we discuss how we can best work together. If the couple lives a great distance from me, we may choose to work primarily by phone and email. Most couples choose to use the material in this book, at least as a starting point. In our initial meeting, we discuss their beliefs, life circumstances, family traditions, and other considerations that affect the kind of wedding they want. I also make it a point to have a discussion about the deeper meaning of marriage in their lives. It is important to most people that the ceremony reflects who they are and what they believe in as individuals and as a couple. Most want it to last from about fifteen minutes to half an hour—long enough to be meaningful and short enough to keep everyone's attention. I usually encourage couples to trust that their own unique style will provide discernment and find its own expression.

Unless a couple has a very specific, alternative approach to creating their wedding, we work with the format presented in Part Two of this book, supplemented by the Sample Ceremonies in Part Three, any readings they would like to include, and the Checklists and Worksheets. With the expectation that the couple will read through and find the specific passages that are right for them after our meeting, my focus here is to educate them about the purposes of the different component parts of the ceremony.

Since the majority of couples I work with have very little idea of how to create their ceremony, this book is designed to expose them to as many ideas as possible. This allows them to recognize that they have a place of discernment inside of them that knows what is right for them and what is not. It is fascinating to witness a couple discovering their ceremony through the process of reacting to all the different options. It's as though they were looking in a mirror and recognizing themselves.

When possible, I like to have the ceremony completed at least a month before the wedding date. This way, it does not become a part of the last-minute flurry of activities. To accomplish that, we set deadlines to complete the rough draft and final draft.

I usually conduct the wedding rehearsal the day before the ceremony. This is covered in detail on pages 52 to 58. In general, I find this to be an important time to meet the families and wedding party and to make sure we share the same understanding about what has to be done, when, where, and by whom during the ceremony. We talk through the logistics and all movements of the wedding party. I try to make it a fun experience, but make sure that doesn't get in the way of doing a thorough job.

In my experience, performing weddings for couples being married outside of any specific religious denomination is one of the true blessings of my ministry. It is an opportunity to truly celebrate our differences and to affirm the universal language of love spoken by all human hearts. I hope those of you who are beginning to or continuing to officiate at these weddings will be as enriched as I have been.

A Final Thought

When all is said and done, and all the guests have gone, you will be left with each other and the day-to-day process of being married to each other. I encourage you to find ways each day to keep your vows alive. Hold yourselves and each other accountable for nourishing your love so that it becomes a source of physical, mental, emotional, and spiritual well-being for you both. What your marriage will become—how it will be for you to wake up each morning beside each other—is entirely up to you now. I wish you the courage to defy the odds and have a great, healthy, happy, and fun marriage. May God bless you always in all ways.

About the Author

Robert K. Johnson

Reverend Judith Johnson, PhD, lives in Rhinebeck, New York. She is an ordained ecumenical minister honoring all religious and spiritual traditions, and has officiated at hundreds of weddings over the past fourteen years. She is a social psychologist maintaining a private practice counseling individuals and families. She also serves as an executive coach and consultant for entrepreneurial and corporate clients. Reverend Johnson holds master's degrees in business administration and spiritual science and a doctorate in social psychology. She is currently working on a second doctorate in spiritual science, focusing on the issue of trust in the divine, ourselves, and each other.